FOR CHRISTIANS

THE SURVIVAL GUIDE

ON CAMPUS

How
to Be
Students
and
Disciples
at the
Same Time

FOR CHRISTIANS

THE SURVIVAL GUIDE

ON CAMPUS

Tony Campolo
William Willimon

HOWARD
PUBLISHING CO.

Our purpose at Howard Publishing is to:

• *Increase faith* in the hearts of growing Christians
• *Inspire holiness* in the lives of believers
• *Instill hope* in the hearts of struggling people everywhere
Because He's coming again!

The Survival Guide for Christians on Campus © 2002
by Tony Campolo and William Willimon
All rights reserved. Printed in the United States of America

Published by Howard Publishing Co., Inc.
3117 North 7th Street, West Monroe, Louisiana 71291-2227

02 03 04 05 06 07 08 09 10 11   10 9 8 7 6 5 4 3 2 1

Edited by Philis Boultinghouse
Interior design by John Luke

ISBN: 1-58229-236-1

DEDICATION

to David Black,
a university president
with a vision for students

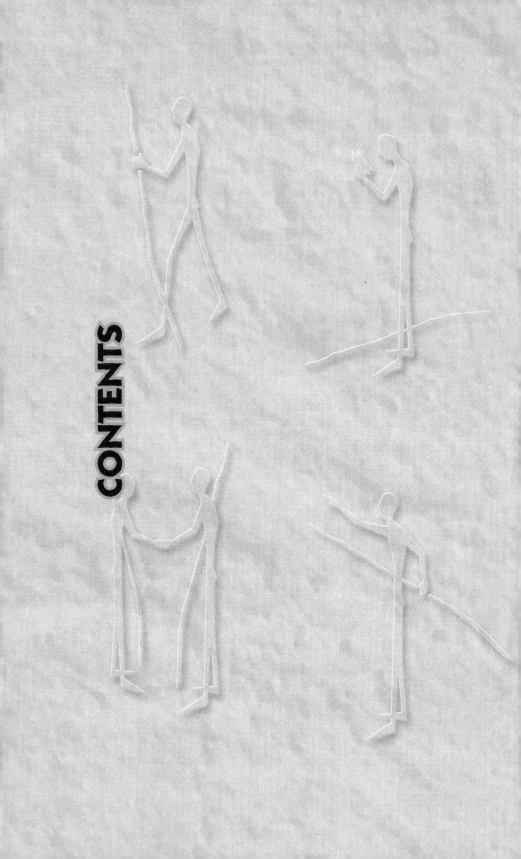

CONTENTS

CONTENTS

ACKNOWLEDGMENTS

ACKNOWLEDGMENTS

Will wants to thank Ms. Jackie Andrews for her accurate and tireless typing.

Tony wants to thank Valerie Hoffmann, who faithfully did his typing; Peggy Campolo, his wife, who did an excellent job of proof reading; and Philis Boultinghouse, for her fantastic editing.

A MESSAGE FROM
TONY AND WILL

A MESSAGE FROM TONY AND WILL

"I used to be a dedicated Christian," said the man looking intently at my teeth. "Then, like a lot of people, I went to college. I took a couple of religion courses that did more to destroy my religion than to teach me anything about it. Those professors asked some tough questions about the Bible and made me see that it's mostly just a bunch of myths and ancient fables. That was the beginning of the end of my faith."

I couldn't say anything to counter his comments with all those dental tools stuck in my mouth. But what I would have said to that dentist if I could have, I now say to you: College can be a place where you grow—not only intellectually, but also spiritually. The Christian faith is not threatened by tough questions, and you don't have to endure a lobotomy to be a believer. Some of the greatest minds that the human race has produced—Paul, Augustine, Blaise Paschal, Soren Kierkegaard,

Dorothy Sayers, Flannery O'Connor, to mention only a few—put tough questions to Jesus and came away more firm in their faith, not less, and more convinced than ever that the narrow way of Christian discipleship was the only way for them to go.

A recent conversation with a college student exemplifies the struggle to maintain faith on a university campus.

"So you are in a campus Bible study?" Will asked.

"Yep," the student answered. "I love my Bible study group. We meet every Wednesday in the basement of the dorm."

"You were big into Bible study in high school?"

"No. I grew up Episcopalian. I don't think we do that sort of stuff."

"Well," Will continued, "I find it interesting that, though you have not been in a Bible study group before, you come here to college and get into Bible study. Why is that?"

He looked at Will as if he were dumb, then said, "Dr. Willimon, have you ever tried to be a sophomore *and* a Christian at the same time? It's not easy."

We expect that many of you know exactly what this sophomore is talking about. Here you are in college for the time of your life, some of the most important years you will ever have, among the world's privileged few who are able to go into higher education. What a great place to be.

And yet, you're also a Christian. The modern college or university campus can be a challenging place for a Christian. Perhaps this is your first time away from home. That means you must learn to get along with roommates, do laundry, spend weekends away from your family. Or perhaps you are one of the growing number of commuter students, having to balance the commute to class, a demanding work schedule, and tight finances. With so much to do, there's not much time left for religious things. Then on the weekends, you have to contend with the sometimes intimidating social scene and the challenges and pressures of dating, drinking, or worse. And then there's church—which has an odd habit of usually meeting at eleven o'clock on a Sunday morning—a very inconvenient time of the week for most college students!

Intellectually, your life is now in the fast lane. You are growing every day, in class and outside of class. You are reading books they never told you about in high school. Your mind is expanding. Almost every day some new insight or idea assaults your consciousness. Will the Christian faith you brought to college be able to hold up under the scrutiny of all you are learning?

The way we see it, God has called you, at this stage in your life, to the ministry of study. Just as God called Moses to lead the Hebrews out of slavery and Paul to preach the gospel to Gentiles, so God has called you to study, grow, and witness on a college campus. Some Christians have as their primary vocation service to others in need. Others serve Christ by witnessing for Him where they work on the assembly line or in the office. Your ministry is as a student on a modern campus. That probably will not be your ministry forever, but right now, the most important thing you can do for Jesus is to study, to use all the intellectual gifts God has given you, to grow in your faith, and to become more steadfast in your commitment to Christ, more disciplined in your faith, and more determined to spend your life walking Christ's way rather than the world's.

The two of us are brash enough to believe that we can help you in your Christian discipleship. We have given most of our lives to working with students in a variety of situations. Both of us are college professors. (Have you ever tried to be a professor *and* a Christian at the same time? It isn't easy.) Tony is a sociologist who has spoken to students on every continent and who has created and supported dozens of social justice ministries for students around the world. Will is a chaplain, preacher, and theologian who has spoken to students around the world, usually in places that wanted Tony but couldn't get on his schedule! Will tries to rescue a few students every year from the clutches of the American upwardly mobile rat race. In a good year, he will get more than a few to go with Jesus. Will is Tony without the caffeine. Tony is Will without the thick southern accent.

We expect that some of the students who read this book are committed Christians who want to *remain* committed Christians while in college. Others of you may not yet think of yourselves as Christians. You are thinking about the Christian faith and exploring the possibility of following Jesus as His disciple. You know some good things about Jesus and the Christian faith, but you are not yet ready to put your money down on Him and follow Him.

We want to speak both to those who have committed to Christ and to those who have not. We want to be helpful to those who have been Christians since childhood and now want to grow in their faith while they are students. We also want to assist those who may know very little about Jesus and His way but are open to learning more about Him and thinking seriously about His claim upon their lives.

You may want to read this book alone, keeping it close at hand, reading it along with all of your other class assignments, perhaps tracking down some of the scripture references as you come across them. Or you may want to get with a group of friends and read and discuss the book together. We think this is the best way to do it. As we will note later in the book, Christianity is a uniquely group experience. Following Jesus is too demanding to do alone. The ideas in this book are meant to be explored together. Why not covenant with a couple of friends to give about ten weeks of the semester to reading this book, along with the Bible. We've provided questions for each chapter to help stimulate your thinking and provoke discussion. (You'll find the questions at the end of the book.)

The Gospels begin with Jesus going forth and calling a group of ordinary, everyday people to follow Him as His disciples. No sooner does Jesus begin to preach "Repent, for the kingdom of heaven has come near" (Matthew 4:17), than He calls ordinary people to help Him. With a simple "Follow me," Jesus calls His disciples to drop what they are doing and walk with Him (Matthew 4:18–22). You might think that, if Jesus is the Son of God, He could do anything He pleased on His own. But that's not the way this Savior works. Jesus is God's way of reclaiming the world, of turning it around, of restoring the beauty and innocence of the original creation. But Jesus does not work alone. He graciously calls ordinary women and men to work with Him. It's as though Jesus is saying, "I'm going to take over the world, and guess who's going to help Me?"

After you read this book, we'd like to hear your reactions to what we've written. Write to Will at Duke (will@duke.edu) or to Tony at Eastern College (1300 Eagle Road, St. Davids, PA 19087) and let us know how this journey was for you.

We believe you are being called by Jesus to join in His saving work. We believe Jesus wants you to join His revolution. We hope this book will help you be true to your vocation, that what we have written here will be a means for you to say, when the call of God comes upon your life, "Here am I. Send me!" (Isaiah 6:8).

1 HOW DO I KNOW IF I'M A CHRISTIAN?

I think I'm a Christian, but I'm not always sure. Some of the people at church tell me that I have to be sure, but I don't know how to do that.

Figuring out who you are and what you believe is part of what the college experience is all about. And although figuring out whether or not you are a Christian has more to do with the *decision* to follow Christ than it does with a *definition* of Christianity, definitions are helpful nonetheless. Christianity begins with a set of *beliefs,* but its real foundation is a *relationship*—a relationship with God and with His Son. This relationship is based on mutual love, and out of that love, Christians choose to *obey* God and to answer His *calling* to live a life that is in many ways contrary to this world.

We'll begin our discussion at the beginning: with *belief.*

◆ BELIEF ◆

Everyone is a believer. That is, everyone lives life on the basis of some set of ideas, some mix of commitments and images. In reality, there is no such thing as a "nonbeliever." Some people think of themselves as nonbelievers; but just let something very wonderful or very terrible happen to them, and their first response is to ask "Why?" or more specifically, "Why did this happen to me?"

And when you answer any "why?" question—"Why is there a world?" or "Why get out of bed in the morning?"—you are on your way to stating your beliefs. There are those whose creed is "Make as much money as you can as quickly as you can." Others have a theology that asserts that there is no such thing as theology, no point to life other than what we ourselves make of it, no voice other than our own. But everyone gets out of bed in the morning for a reason. We all live life on the basis of some set of convictions, some "creed."

Ask someone on your campus who is knocking him- or herself out for perfect grades, "Why are you doing this?" and you are likely to hear something like, "Because I believe…"

Christians believe that the answer to our most interesting questions, our deepest questions, tends to be "Jesus." Ask us, "What is the point of life?" and we'll respond, "Following Jesus."

Beliefs make us who we are and provide perspective on what's going on in the world.

Everyone is a believer.

Basic Christian Beliefs

In many churches, Christians recite the Apostles' Creed as

part of their worship. This creed emerged in its earliest forms during the first century to define orthodox doctrines for the church, which already was struggling against heresies. While not divinely inspired like the Bible, this creed is a good place for us to begin our quest to figure out what Christians believe and to help you decide whether or not you really are one. For a concise statement of what is at the core of what Christians believe, it can't be beat!

The Apostles' Creed

I believe in God the Father Almighty, maker of heaven and earth; and in Jesus Christ His only Son our Lord; who was conceived by the Holy Ghost; born of the Virgin Mary; suffered under Pontius Pilate; was crucified, dead, and buried; He descended into hell; The third day He rose again from the dead; He ascended into heaven; and sitteth on the right hand of God the Father Almighty; from thence He shall come to judge the quick and the dead.

I believe in the Holy Ghost; the holy catholic ["catholic," here, means "universal"] church; the communion of saints; the forgiveness of sins; the resurrection of the body; and the life everlasting. Amen.

Right off the bat, the creed tells us that Christians believe in a God who is a loving parent. (The word *father* in the ancient language of Jesus' world was *Abba*, which is an affectionate ascription like our word *daddy*.) Christians believe that we have a God who loves us more than any earthly mother or father ever could. So great is His love for us that God wants to be personally involved in our lives. That's why Jesus came into the world (John 3:16).

We believe that, in order to show infinite love for us, God became one of us (John 1:14). We believe that, two thousand years ago, the Creator of the universe actually became a human being, grew up in a place called Nazareth, and changed the course of human history. We further believe that only by becoming one of us could God show, in a way that we could even begin to grasp, the greatness of His incredible love for us. Only because God came to us in Jesus, can we come to God (Hebrews 2:14–15).

Only through His incarnation did it become possible for us to know God's love for us.

Perhaps a story will provide a little help in understanding why God's becoming a human being is so much a part of what we Christians believe:

There was once, in the land of make-believe, a man who loved ants. He had an anthill in his backyard, and every day he would go and spread food for the ants to eat. He gave them sugar and pieces of bread and crumbs from cookies. As the ants came out and took the food to carry back to the anthill, he would yell at them, "Ants, I love you! Ants, I love you!" But the ants never caught the message. How could they? He was a man, and they were ants—two different species that did not speak the same language.

In this make-believe story, the man had magical powers. He could turn himself into anything. So he did the obvious thing to do if he wanted to communicate with ants: He turned himself into one of them and went in among them to tell them the good news. "Fellow ants: That huge creature that hovers over you and at times frightens you is a man who loves you. He is the one who provides you with all of the good food you eat. He cares for you day in and day out."

The other ants were curious about how he knew so much about the big creature that had frightened them. So the special ant explained, "I am that creature. I became one of you because it was the only way I could tell you about myself and how much I love you."

You see, God *had* to become one of us; He had to be *incarnate,* meaning "in the flesh." Only through His incarnation did it become possible for us to know God's love for us. Furthermore, as the Creed says, we believe that the ultimate expression of that love was when Jesus suffered for us. As Jesus Himself said, "No one has greater love than this, to lay down one's life for one's friends" (John 15:13). This concept is far beyond our understanding, but we Christians claim that through His death, Jesus provided for our salvation.

The most common explanation of what really happened

during the crucifixion of Jesus is called the Penal-Substitutionary Doctrine of the Atonement. What this theologically jargoned phrase means is that somehow, as Jesus was tortured to death on a hill outside Jerusalem, He took upon Himself the punishment that each and every one of us deserves because of our sins and the kind of people we've allowed ourselves to become (1 Peter 2:24). Christians believe that in some mysterious way Jesus went through hell on our behalf. Jesus died a horrible, bloody death at our hands. Any God who would come to us in human form and who was willing to shed His blood and endure great pain in order to save us from our sins must love us very much. It must be painful for the Creator to love creatures like us.

If all of this seems a bit weird to you, don't feel dismayed. The Bible, out of which Christians get this seemingly scandalous belief, acknowledges how hard it is to grasp the idea of the cross as our salvation. One verse in the Bible reads: "For the message about the cross is foolishness to those who are perishing, but to us who are being saved it is the power of God" (1 Corinthians 1:18).

In a culture that worships power, pleasure, and self-sufficiency, the concept that God became known to us through weakness, suffering, and service is downright shocking!

The Importance of the Bible

Every part of the Apostles' Creed is based on the Bible, and we Christians take the Bible very seriously: We take it to be a truthful message from God. Once, while Tony was lecturing at an Ivy League university, a student asked him in an incredulous tone of voice, "How can you believe the Bible? You seem like a reasonable person, and apparently you are well educated. So how can you believe all those myths and fables?"

"Well, first of all," Tony explained, "the Bible is not a collection of myths and fables. But more to the point—I believe this book because I decided to! Some time ago, there was a day when I decided to believe what the Bible said about Jesus. Ever since then, I've been assembling arguments and justifications to support what I decided to believe."

Tony could see that his grand inquisitor was taken back by the frankness of his answer. The intelligent student knew it would be impossible for Tony to validate with empirical proofs the claims he had made about the Bible, but Tony beat him to the draw with the simple acknowledgement that he was a believer because of an existential commitment.

But Tony wasn't going to let that student get away without an acknowledgment on his part that *he* had no empirical proof to support his rejection of the Bible. So he said to the young man, "Now that I've told you why I believe the Bible, I would like you to tell me why you *don't* believe it. Isn't it because you *decided* not to? Didn't you make up your mind some time ago that the Bible was nothing but myths and fairy tales, and haven't you been assembling arguments and justifications to support your disbelief ever since?"

It's hard to win such arguments. Tony's intent at that moment was to create a level playing field, to make it clear to the audience that disbelief is as empirically ungrounded as belief. The young questioner probably had not read much of the Bible. His disbelief was the result of his own decision to believe that the negative things others had told him about the Bible were true. And that decision probably had made it impossible for him to do any serious reading of the Book.

The Value of a Support Group

We must first understand the social factors influencing belief in order to understand why Christians believe what they do and also what sustains their convictions. Peter Berger, one of the most popular writers in the field of sociology, contends that the maintenance of a belief system is primarily possible because of the support of what he calls "a plausibility structure." What Berger means is that usually belief is maintained because the believer has a primary reference group that regularly reaffirms, revitalizes, or reinforces belief. What is real is whatever a person is told is real by the significant others in his or her life.

Suppose you were marooned on an isolated island in the Pacific along with 150 indigenous islanders. Imagine that they all thought you were handsome and constantly told you that you were. With no other voice expressing opposition to their definition of handsome, how long do you suppose it would be before you believed what they were telling you, despite any imperfections in your appearance? The islanders would become your plausibility structure, and if you were with them for long, it is likely that in time you would come to believe what they told you about yourself.

Now, we're not suggesting that believing in God is to be equated with believing a judgment about your good looks, but we *are* saying that belief in God, like belief in anything else, requires a plausibility structure if it is to be sustained over an extended period of time. The new Christian must learn quickly that being a person of faith is no task for lone rangers. If you are going to survive as a Christian, it is essential that you form a plausibility structure to help you to maintain your belief system.

Tony has such a group. The four of them get together once a week, usually very early on Tuesday mornings at a coffee shop. These four men are good friends.

The new Christian must learn quickly that being a person of faith is no task for lone rangers.

They talk about what's going on in their lives and share how they have fared spiritually during the previous week. They reinforce one another's faith commitments and do their best to lend the kind of mutual support that can keep faith alive and vital. Christianity is a group thing.

Whenever college students ask what they should do to sustain their faith in light of the onslaught of secular thinking that pervades the modern campus, Tony always tells them, "Become part of a good group." This group can be their plausibility structure. The best support groups meet regularly so members can check up on each other's spiritual journeys and reaffirm for each other that being a believer is not a crazy thing. Otherwise, the college setting can make Christianity seem crazy.

To tell the truth, everyone is a member of some group that provides a plausibility structure. It may be the biology department that regularly tells you that you are a descendant of primordial slime. It may be a fraternity that teaches you that you have no greater calling than to get drunk and be the life of the party. Some group or another will provide a plausibility structure for you. Nobody ever *really* thinks for him- or herself. So the issue is not "Will I be a member of a group who tells me how to think?" but rather "Will the group that tells me how to think be committed to biblical truth?"

Jesus Himself had a support group, thus modeling what all of His followers should do. Most of us can name the three disciples who were in His support group. They were Peter, James, and John. These were the "brothers" who were with Him on the Mount of Transfiguration when Jesus went through the most magnificent theophany in history (Matthew 17:1–8). They were with Him in the Garden of Gethsemane just before His death, when He needed their reinforcement for the ordeal of

Calvary (Matthew 26:36–46). Because Jesus, being human as well as being God, depended so much on their support and encouragement, you can only imagine how disappointed He must have been when they fell asleep during the hour in which He went through His greatest emotional struggles.

If Jesus needed a support group to strengthen Him, what makes any Christian think that he or she can do without one? You need a group if you are to have the assurance that you really are a Christian.

Dealing with Doubt

Even if you are a part of a good support group and have a firm belief, you should know that times of doubt are part of the ongoing life of every Christian. A multitude of factors can disrupt our faith and fill our hearts with doubt.

Unexplained tragedy. When you can't find answers to the question of "Why?" doubt may begin to drift slowly but surely into your consciousness.

Physical and spiritual fatigue. Sometimes we become vulnerable to doubt as a result of physical fatigue. We get worn out trying to do too much and failing to take time out for rest. College students, who sometimes fail to observe good health habits and are too often sleep deprived, may be particularly susceptible to a sort of spiritual fatigue that nurtures doubt.

Chemical imbalances. Imbalances in the chemistry of the body also can be doubt inducing. Be careful not to confuse a physiological condition with a spiritual condition.

Disappointment. Disappointment in someone you trust can give rise to doubt. The unfaithfulness of a mate or the moral "fall" of a respected clergyperson may do it. Spiritual doubt often comes when you are disillusioned by people whom you thought of as "godly models."

Spiritual warfare. Those in the Pentecostal and charismatic versions of Christianity sometimes contend that doubt is a consequence of being under attack from dark, evil spirits. They see doubt as a demonic force and call upon Christians to "take up the whole armor of God" (Ephesians 6:13) as they engage in spiritual warfare against this dark force. The intellectual elite sometimes dismiss such talk in cavalier fashion, but in this postmodern era, some sophisticated members of the intelligentsia are giving a second thought to such an explanation for doubt. Sometimes doubt really feels like being under attack by something or someone outside ourselves.

We both believe that doubt is part of the normative experience of every Christian. Carlyle Marney, one of the great preachers in America's history, confessed that there were some days when he didn't "believe" at all. Tennyson said, "There is more faith in honest doubt than in half the creeds!"

Those who take their believing seriously struggle to interpret all of life from the perspective of their faith commitments, and this is not always easy. There are so many unanswered questions and so many incredible claims in the Scriptures that there are times when those who think deeply can be overwhelmed by it all. In *The Tragic Sense of Life in Men and Nations*, the Spanish existentialist Miguel Unomuno once said: "Those who believe they believe in God, but without passion in their hearts, without anguish of mind, without uncertainty, without doubt, and even at times without despair, believe only in the idea of God, but not in God himself." Persons who struggle with doubt and work through it to a reaffirmation of faith are likely to come out stronger in their convictions than ever before.

But we must take care that our doubt is *honest doubt*. Sometimes doubt is a cover-up for something else—specifically, sin. As Blaise Pascal once said, "There is a doubt that comes from disobedience." For instance, a collegian grows up in a religious tradition that considers sex outside of marriage a sin against God. But this particular young man starts having sex with a woman on campus who seems more than willing to have sex without any kind of commitment. Immediately, he begins to feel guilt or, for those who are into psycho babble, "cognitive dissonance." He begins to suffer from inner tensions that arise because of the conflict between his moral convictions and his behavior.

There are two ways to resolve such cognitive dissonance. One is for the young man to repent and bring his behavior into harmony with his beliefs. But if he enjoys the sex too much, he just might take the opposite course and resolve his inner tension by ridding himself of the God he believes condemns his actions. The doubt that comes from such mental gymnastics is not honest doubt. It is unfair for that student to say, "I reject belief in God because I have found theism to be untenable." In reality, he rejects God because he is sleeping with his girlfriend and cannot reconcile his behavior with belief in the God who forbids that behavior.

❖ RELATIONSHIP ❖

Believing in biblical truths is an intellectual thing; being a Christian is much more than that. Being a Christian involves having a personal relationship with Jesus. This is possible because we believe that after being buried for three days, Jesus rose from the grave and came back to life (1 Corinthians 15:1–7). Not only did He come back to life, but Jesus came back to the very disciples who had forsaken Him. After appearing several times to His disciples and to enough others to provide sufficient witnesses to verify that He had indeed returned from the dead, Jesus ascended into heaven, even as the Bible says (Acts 1:9). And we believe the Bible to be a truthful rendition of what really happened as Jesus rose from the dead and came back to us.

Christians believe that Jesus is still present with us. He promised to come back as the Holy Spirit (the third member of the Trinity) and to be ever present with us (Matthew 28:20). We believe that Jesus is present within every Christian—within you—even as you read this. Furthermore, we declare that anyone who is open to the Holy Spirit can have a personal encounter with Jesus right now!

Each morning Tony tries to wake up earlier than he has to in order to do a special kind of praying. He doesn't ask God for anything. Instead, he just lies in bed in absolute stillness and says the name of Jesus over and over again to himself. He does this to keep his mind from wandering off to the thousand things that need to be done that day. In the early morning still-

Believing in biblical truths is an intellectual thing; being a Christian is much more than that.

ness, Tony subjectively surrenders to the invisible presence of Jesus, open to an invasion by His Holy Spirit.

This sounds quite mystical. That's because it is! Having a personal relationship with an invisible, resurrected Jesus hardly fits into the canons of science and rationality; but in our increasingly postmodern world, it seems less and less strange. This living, ever deepening relationship with Jesus is at the core of what Christians mean by being "born again."

Tony experiences this relationship in solitude and stillness. Will tends to experience it through liturgy in a traditional church service. Some meet Jesus most vividly in their work with the poor and suffering. Still others give testimonies of having subjective encounters with Jesus through highly charged evangelistic rallies such as those conducted by Billy Graham.

For some, encounters with Jesus are full of disruptive emotion. For others, surrendering to Jesus is more of a thoughtful, peaceful transition in life. But each one of us comes to a point, either suddenly or through a long process, where we become aware that a transition has occurred and a new definition of "self" has been secured. We know that we are not alone.

If you've never done this—if you've never inwardly yielded to the unseen presence of the resurrected Jesus—you may want to do it right now. You may want to find a quiet place and there inwardly decide to be open to Jesus. Then give Him time to possess you. Maybe you'll feel something, and maybe you won't. But surrender is the place to start. Don't be reluctant to tell Jesus that the next step is His. And don't be reluctant to ask some committed Christian to give you advice and help in this venture. On the cross, Jesus went through so much to get to you. We are, therefore, confident that He will do what's needed to get to you now.

✧ OBEDIENCE ✧

As a boy in Sunday School, Tony often sang the old gospel song "Trust and Obey."

Not a shadow can rise,

Not a cloud in the skies,

But His smile quickly drives it away;

Not a doubt nor a fear,

Not a sigh nor a tear,

Can abide while we trust and obey.

At first read, the song may seem trite; but as Tony has reflected on it of late, he has realized that there is profound meaning in this hymn. Trusting (or believing) in Jesus and obeying God's directives for life, as set forth in the Bible, are required of the Christian. The two go together! Obedience follows the realization that what Jesus did on the cross, He did for you. As you realize that Jesus loved you so much that if you were the only person in human history, He still would have died just for you, you are obligated to say, "After what He did for me, there isn't anything I wouldn't do for Him!" You want to express your gratitude for His gift, purchased at so great a price. Jesus lets you know that you can do that by obeying Him. He says, "If you love me, you will keep my commandments" (John 14:15).

Clear Biblical Teaching

Some of the things Jesus wants you to do are written down in the Bible. For instance, He tells us not to return evil for evil but to do good to those who would hurt us. This is one of many biblical directives that are quite clear. It's easy to understand, but tough to do. People try to get around such clear demands of the Bible. When W. C. Fields, the famous comedian, was in a hospital bed near death, his wife was surprised to find her agnostic husband reading the Bible. When she exclaimed, "W. C.! What are you doing?" he answered in his inimitable manner, "Looking for loopholes, my dear, looking for loopholes!"

Many times people complain that the Bible isn't more specific about certain ethical issues like abortion or capital punishment. But let's be honest. Even where the Bible does speak very clearly, our problem is not misunderstanding, but rather, unwillingness to obey.

As G. K. Chesterton, the brilliant English journalist whose arguments against the agnostic George Bernard Shaw regularly made the front page of the London Times, once said, "We might have a good debate on whether or not Jesus believed in the existence of fairies. Who knows? Jesus said nothing, so far as we know, about fairies. But we can have no debate on whether or not Jesus believed that rich people were in big trouble. There's plenty in the Bible on that subject."

> **Our problem is not misunderstanding, but rather, unwillingness to obey.**

When God's Will Isn't So Clear

It is amazing how many things the Bible specifically requires of us. It addresses so many of the questions about what we should and should not do. However, there are some things that we are expected to figure out for ourselves. Many Christians address such concerns simply by asking themselves, "What Would Jesus Do?" As they think through the answers to this question, they believe they have figured out the will of God. To remind themselves always to ask this question before making decisions, some Christians, especially new Christians, wear bracelets, pins, or shirts with "WWJD" on them. They want reminders that, as Christians, they must be committed to doing what Jesus would do if He were in their particular situation. In order to honestly answer the question those four letters ask, it is necessary to spend a lot of time reading the four Gospels and reflecting on the kind of person the historical Jesus must have been. Many Christians try hard to imagine what Jesus would do if He were faced with what they have to face day in and day out. To do so, you must know as much about Jesus as you can. Just closing your eyes and saying "WWJD" without putting substantial biblical support in it is pointless.

When you really get down to it, there is some guesswork in all of this. Perhaps that is why the Bible says, "Work out your own salvation with fear and trembling" (Philippians 2:12). This verse suggests that, even when you work hard to figure out what you think Jesus would do in your place, you shouldn't be so arrogant as to think you can't be wrong. But if you really *are* seeking God's will, your seeking must be pleasing to Jesus.

It's not as though you have no help in all your decision-making. When Jesus ascended into heaven after His resurrection, He promised He would send the Holy Spirit and that the Spirit would be a "counselor" to guide us (John 14:26 NIV). That means that the third member of the Trinity is always ready to provide you with inner promptings as to what you should or should not do. But remember, even when you feel such promptings, you can never be absolutely sure it is the Holy Spirit working in you. That's why the Bible says to "test the spirits to see whether they are from God" (1 John 4:1). The best way to do such testing is to go back to that support group we talked about earlier. The other members of your group can help you to determine what is of God and what might be your own wishful thinking. God can use them to provide more objective judgments of what Jesus would do if He were in your place.

Experiencing God through Obedience

Obeying what you believe to be the will of God can provide much assurance that you really are a Christian. *Doing does influence feelings.* We are all aware that what we do is highly influenced by what we feel, but often we are not quite so conscious of the fact that what we do can impact how we feel. This translates into a simple principle: The more you do what God wants you to do, the more you will feel God as a reality in your life.

In Mark 10, we read about a young man who comes running up to Jesus wanting assurance of eternal life. Jesus tells him to sell all that he has, give it to the poor, and join His ragtag band of followers. Jesus tells this rich young ruler to do this not only because the poor need help but because Jesus knows what will happen to the young man if he obeys Jesus' directive. Jesus knows that giving sacrificially to the poor will alter the consciousness of this wealthy young man and give him an inner awareness of having surrendered his heart to his new Lord.

Time and time again, collegians have asked us how to get rid of their inner doubts. We tend to tell them to do two things: First, read a lot of Bible because, in ways we don't understand, we know that as they read the Bible, God's Holy Spirit will bear witness to their spirits that they really are children of God (Romans 8:16). Second, we tell them to get involved in some form of Christian ministry. Tony often asks a doubting collegian to come to work as a missionary with his kids in the inner-city ministries in places like Camden, New Jersey. Tony tells them that the more they play games with the boys and girls in the city's government housing projects, the more they listen to the life stories of these children, and the more they talk to them about Jesus, the more they will experience the reality of God's Spirit in their lives. What they *do* will impact how they *feel*, and Tony knows that by doing these things, it won't be long before these young people will have the inner assurance that they belong to Jesus. Will tells them to get involved in a Christian group on campus that can help them put their faith into practice. Christianity is meant to be lived, not just discussed. The more you live the faith, the more faith you are given.

Tony met two students following a lecture at Manchester University in England. They were intrigued by the stories Tony had told about his programs among "at risk" city kids, about the high school dropouts who were nurtured into productive lives, and about the children who started to smile again after years of abuse because now they felt loved. After hearing what Tony had to say, these two students wanted to come to America and work in his programs. They wanted to make their work a part of a field-work assignment for their sociology degrees. However, they thought it only fair to let Tony know that while they had once been believers, they had lost their faith and were no longer Christians. In short, they were asking if he would accept a couple of agnostics as missionaries.

The more you live the faith, the more faith you are given.

Tony told them that they could come and work with him, but only under certain conditions. First and foremost, he told them they had to *act* like Christians. They would be expected to turn up at team Bible studies, attend church on Sundays, tell Bible stories to the kids in the day-camp programs, join in singing gospel songs at assemblies, and constantly try to act as they thought Jesus would act.

We probably do not have to tell you what happened over the next six months. You can guess! By *acting* like Christians, they came to know the real Jesus and were gradually transformed into *being* Christians. In taking on Christian habits, they became Christians. One of them actually decided to go into the pastoral ministry. The actions of these young people impacted and changed what they thought and felt. Whether you are subjectively convinced that you really are a Christian or not has a lot to do with whether or not you obey God's call to lovingly serve other people. Just do it! The feelings can come later.

❖ CALLING ❖

Estranged from Culture

The more you obey the requisites of Scripture and seek to be the kind of person who follows Jesus, the more you will find yourself out of step with the expectations prescribed by the dominant culture. On most college campuses today, Christians are called to be misfits. The apostle Paul has said to Christians: "I appeal to you therefore, brothers and sisters, by the mercies of God, to present your bodies as a living sacrifice, holy and acceptable to God, which is your spiritual worship. Do not be conformed to this world, but be transformed by the renewing of your minds, so that you may discern what is the will of God—what is good and acceptable and perfect" (Romans 12:1–2).

Christians are called to march out of step with their peers and march to the beat of the Distant Drummer—not conformed, but transformed.

Most of us have heard of the movie *Buffy the Vampire Slayer.* The film is about a rah-rah, high-school girl who realizes that she is heir to a calling to slay vampires who are invading her neighborhood and school, sucking blood out of people and making them into "the living dead." She discovers that her unique calling is something that the other kids in her high school cannot relate to or even believe. She tries to go back and be just another kid in the school, but it doesn't work. She tries to be an ordinary teenager who goes out on dates and to parties—but she can't. Little by little she realizes that she has a mission in life that sets her apart from others. Her "calling" makes her different, and she knows she can never again go back to the way she was.

So we say, right up front, that the more you become a Christian, the more estrangement you'll experience. Others around you will pursue their life goals in culturally prescribed ways. For them, education will be the means to get the credentials that will get the jobs that will get the money that will get the things they think they need to be part of the American mainstream culture. But little by little, you will realize that you are different. Early on, the Christian must begin to

The more you become a Christian, the more estrangement you'll experience.

sense that his or her life belongs to Jesus. Your selection of a major and a vocation will be influenced by new criteria. The Christian constantly asks, "What can I do with my life to touch others with the love of the Jesus whom I have come to love?

And what can I do to be an agent of change who will help transform this world into the kind of world God wants it to be?"

Sacrificial Value System

Christians have a different value system. Whereas many in our consumerist society will define themselves in terms of the things they can buy, the Christian will opt, more and more, for a lifestyle that shows concern for the needy of the world. Christians gradually recognize that they are part of an affluent society that enjoys extravagant opulence while most people in the world suffer without their basic needs being met. Hence, Christians gravitate more and more toward believing that they should live simply so that others might simply live. In 1 John 3:17–18, the writer of this scripture asks: "How does God's love abide in anyone who has the world's goods and sees a brother or sister in need and yet refuses help? Little children, let us love, not in word or speech, but in truth and action."

Nearly two thousand verses in Scripture call us to respond sacrificially to the needs of the poor, and the Christian who is obedient to Scripture soon finds that these verses have life-changing implications.

In the movie *A Civil Action*, a lawyer, whose crusade against corporate polluters leaves him penniless, finds himself facing a bankruptcy judge. She can't believe that his only assets are fourteen dollars and a portable radio. "Where are the things by which one measures one's life?" she asks.

For those who belong to the dominant culture, the question is a pertinent one. But for the Christian, the question is ludicrous. The Christian is a counter-culture person, a misfit who measures life in terms of loving service to others and justice achieved for the poor and the oppressed. For the Christian, the only applause that matters comes from nail-pierced hands. Being a Christian is a bold venture. Are you ready for it? Let's go!

2 HOW CAN I READ THE BIBLE AND GET SOMETHING OUT OF IT?

I've tried reading the Bible, but frankly, I just don't get much out of it. It all seems so strange. I have to plow through so much to get to anything that is relevant to my life. I really feel guilty about it because, if you are a Christian, you're supposed to get something out of reading the Bible, right?

"What is the strangest thing we do on Sunday morning?" Will asked a group of Duke students while in conversation with them about Sunday chapel worship.

"It's when the choir files in, and they bring in that great big book," said a student.

"Do you mean the Bible?"

"Yeah, that. And then a person in the procession opens it, puts it on the lectern, and looks toward the clergy, like he or she is saying, 'Here, work from this.'"

And Will thought to himself, *He's right, that* is *weird.*

It is very strange that a group of twenty-first century North Americans would gather and sit silently while someone reads from a great big ancient book, produced in a culture other than our own, in a language quite different from ours. It is strange because we are modern people. We like to think that we live at the summit of human development and stand in sovereign judgment of everybody who got here before we did. That we should gather around and be attentive to any source of wisdom other than that which is contemporary and self-derived *is* weird.

Christians, like Jews, are people of a book. We are members of a community that has been evoked by reading words called Scripture.

Christians differ from Buddhists or Jews or Muslims mainly in that we have listened to different stories. Think of Scripture as a truthful story about how the world came to be, what the world is, and where the world is headed. Scripture is God's story of what life means and why we are here. Christians are none other than people who have had their lives shaped by reading, and then by submitting to, the Good News that is the story of Jesus Christ.

Scripture is God's story of what life means and why we are here.

In just a couple of centuries, the Church defeated the Roman Empire without raising an army, without firing a shot. The Church assembled itself not by the conventional means of gathering by race, gender, or social class, the way the world groups people, but rather through the Word. The Church defeated Rome on the basis of nothing more than a rather disordered group of writings that we have come to call the Bible. Today, the main way the church is formed, the primary way that God gets to us in Jesus Christ, is through Scripture.

❖ THE CHALLENGE OF READING THE BIBLE ❖

It isn't surprising that many people find the Bible tough to read and understand. The Bible is not one book but a whole library, a collection of many writings assembled over a thousand-year period. Its earliest parts were written more than three thousand years ago, and its most recent parts are nearly two thousand years old. The culture of the ancient Near East was quite different from our own. The Hebrew Bible was written in the Hebrew language. (We've used the term "Hebrew Bible" here because Jewish students are sometimes offended when we refer to their Scriptures as the *Old* Testament. To keep from offending them, we should try to use their wording and say, "the Hebrew Bible.") The New Testament was written in Greek. Both of these languages are quite different from English.

In your college classes you have learned that you cannot simply pick up the *Odyssey* of Homer and "get it." It helps to be told the context of what you are reading, its background, and most importantly, its purpose. Parts of the Bible are even older than the *Odyssey*. That's one of the reasons it is difficult to simply pick up the Bible and expect an immediate correlation between the meaning of the Bible in its historical context and what it might say to us today. Parts of the Hebrew Scriptures seem to condone polygamy and slavery. Few today believe these are appropriate practices for Christians. Some Scripture reflects the customs and mores of biblical times more than eternal, divine commands for us. It is, therefore, important to get help in reading Scripture.

The Bible Is Not Immediately Accessible

We abuse Scripture when we expect an immediate, one-to-one correlation between our problems today and the problems addressed by the Bible. In other words, remember that there is quite some distance between the Bible and us. The Bible praises King Solomon as one of the wisest people who ever lived (1 Kings 4:30), yet Solomon had many, many wives. Should our president? One of the skills required of Christians is the ability to read the Bible expecting to hear God's truth while at the same time realizing that God's truth may not be immediately evident. To say that the Bible is "God's Word" does not mean that every word is straight from the mouth of God. The Bible is a product of inspired people. Sometimes the inspiration is more evident in one portion of Scripture than in another. Prayerful, humble, intelligent discernment is required for God's Word, the ancient Scripture, to become God's Word for us today.

We live in a world of instant oatmeal, one-hour dry cleaning, and quickie sex. We want our truth upon demand, instantly, without risk or cost on our part. Understanding the Bible takes time. You already know that any true friendship takes time. In order to be someone's good friend, you must spend time with that person in conversation, in work, in play, and in just hanging out together.

The Bible Is God's Attempt to Get through to Us

Don't think of the Bible primarily as a rule book where you go to get directives for every single step of your life or as a magical source of instant inspiration; rather, think of the Bible as the major means God has provided for us to become friends with Him. Your Bible study, alone or in a group of fellow Christians, is not a legalistic demand or another homework assignment; it is the way you spend time becoming a friend of God.

When you read biology in preparation for your exam, you are looking for facts, for formulas and insights you need to spit back on the exam. When you read about the French Revolution for your course in European history, you are reading for dates, names, places, and insights that will help you better understand this event. There is a little biology in the Bible and a great deal of history, but when you read the Bible, your purpose is far loftier than merely mastering facts and figures. You read the Bible in order to allow the revelation of God to unfold in your life, so that you may be a more faithful disciple of Jesus and better understand the nature of the world as the promised Kingdom of God.

✧ THE BIBLE'S CHALLENGE ✧

Some of the Bible's meaning is quickly apparent, readily available to the casual reader—but not much of it. The Bible is mostly about God and His will for the world, whereas we tend to be concerned mainly with ourselves. We must take time with the Bible, study it, contextualize it, memorize it, take it to heart. That's one reason we gather on Sundays, once a week, to listen to the Bible, because the story it tells is so counter to the world's stories, so against our natural inclinations, that we must go over it again and again, week after week, in order to get the point. The good news is that Christianity is a "revealed religion" because we have a God who seems eager to be revealed to us. The Bible is, in great part, a long, wonderful story of God's relentless determination to reveal His purposes and love for us. The stories of the patriarchs and matriarchs of Israel, the stunning words of the prophets, the poetry of the psalms, the words and work of Jesus, the cross, the letters of Paul, the visions of Revelation—all

> **The Bible can also be used by us to further our own selfish agendas.**

of this we believe to be the creative, resourceful attempt of God to get through to us.

But let's be honest. The problem is not so much that the Bible is old and we are modern or that the Bible is intentionally obscure; it is rather that the Bible is true, whereas we tend to be deceitful. The real problem is that what the Bible urges upon us is difficult!

The Bible Demands Transformation

Most of us are fairly content with our lives as they are. Change is painful for us. We don't want to let go of the old and embrace the new. The Bible's goal is not mere understanding or agreement. The Bible demands *transformation*. We live in a world that urges us to "make up your own mind." The Bible seeks to form our minds.

We live in a world that tells us, "The new is good, the old is bad." The Bible wants to bend our lives to the ancient wisdom of the saints.

We tend to hear what we want to hear, to hear that which corresponds with our preconceptions and prejudices. The Bible lures us toward another world, God's world.

One of Shakespeare's characters notes that "the Devil quotes Scripture for his own purposes." The Bible can also be used by us to further our own selfish agendas. We can rummage about in the Bible, using dislocated proof texts to make some point that is more our belief than God's truth. We are sinful creatures who are capable of using any of God's good gifts, even the gift of Scripture, to further our own selfish ends. The point of reading the Bible is to allow it to *remake* our lives rather than *justify* our lives.

Conversion, not simply information, is the goal of our reading. We read the Bible as our contribution to the continuing process of our being born again and again and again. One of the fun things that happens when you read the Bible regularly is that you can read a passage that you have read maybe a hundred times before—but this time, as you read, something jumps out at you, grabs you by the collar, shakes you up and down, and demands to be heard in a fresh, new way.

Many of us have the habit of going to the Bible, seeking the answer to this or that question—"searching the Scriptures," we call it. But the longer we read the Bible, the more we realize that the Scriptures are about the business of questioning and examining us. "Thou has searched me and known me," says the psalmist. Therefore, when we read the Bible, our question ought not simply be, "Do I agree with this?" but rather, "How is this biblical passage asking me to change?"

As someone has said, it is not that we have tried Christianity and found it incomprehensible. The problem is that we have tried Christianity and found it difficult! Our problem is not that there are vast portions of Scripture that we don't understand; our problem is that there are many portions of

Scripture that we understand all too well! We know that these verses demand transformation, change, detoxification, and conversion—and that can be painful.

The Bible Is about *Everything*

Our lives are formed by the stories to which we listen. Every day the world's stories are having their way with us.

"Buy a lot of Pepsi, get a lot of stuff."

"You've got the whole world in your hands—MasterCard."

"Everybody in denim—The Gap."

The Bible is not just a book about religion. The Bible is about *everything*. The Bible wants *all* of us, Monday through Sunday. In reading the Bible, we are asked to relinquish the tight grip of the world's officially approved stories in order to be embraced solely by God's story.

The Bible is better than a book of rules. It is a way of transferring us into a new world, of bringing us, step by step, closer to the Kingdom of God. Now we see God and His kingdom "in a mirror, dimly," as Paul says in 1 Corinthians 13:12, "but then we will see face to face." One day, that which the Bible has been trying so resourcefully to show us will be fully visible. We shall know as we have been known. God

> The Bible is not just a book about religion. The Bible is about *everything*.

will be all in all, and we will be, in the words of the Wesleyan hymn, "Lost in wonder, love, and praise."

Think of the Bible, not as a road map that will tell you every single step to take in life, but rather as a compass that keeps truthfully pointing you in the right direction. "Your word is a lamp to my feet," says the psalmist. In this light, we see the Light of Life.

❖ RULES FOR READING ❖

Here are some of our suggestions for your Bible reading:

Read the Bible with Others

The Bible was produced by the Church, for the Church. Many faithful hands, from many different historical periods, have given us the Bible. There are many voices in Scripture, many different perspectives. After all, the Bible is talking about God, and it is as if, to be faithful to the subject, we need the testimony and insight of many different witnesses. The Bible is not meant to be read exclusively sitting by yourself, but in common with other struggling believers. The interpretations, corrections, and challenges offered by reading the Bible in communion with our fellow Christians are essential. Those portions of Scripture that you find difficult to understand may be the most beloved by your sister or brother. Your cherished interpretations may need enrichment and cultivation by the gifts and insights of others. If you aren't in a Bible study group, get in one now!

Read the Bible as a Means of Communion with God

You spend years learning how to read history, plays, or chemistry. Each subject requires different methods of reading, different sorts of interpretive questions. When we read history, our main question might be, "How did this event really happen?" When we read about biology, we might ask, "Is this an accurate depiction of the organic processes whereby this life form evolved?" The Bible, generally speaking, always and everywhere, talks primarily about God and only secondarily or derivatively about anything else. The major concerns of the Bible are theological—not historical, scientific, or mathematical. So the Bible delights in figurative, metaphorical, and poetic language, because that kind of language best moves our hearts and expresses matters that are difficult to articulate. When the Bible says that Jesus "descended into the lower parts of the earth" (Ephesians 4:9), it doesn't mean that He traveled to the molten core of our planet, but rather that He entered into the inner sanctum of the Evil One. When the Bible speaks in Isaiah 55 of the trees clapping their hands and the stars singing together in Job 38, enjoy the poetry; don't worry about the biology or astronomy. We are not to treat the Bible as some sort of object, a cadaver on a table that we are to pick apart. Rather, our Bible reading is a kind of conversation, a dialogue between us and God, a conversation between those who have attempted to be faithful to God in the past and those of us who are attempting to be faithful to God in the present.

As we've said earlier, the Bible is the major means by which we become friends with God.

Read the Bible Regularly

Keep at it. As we say, it takes time—a lifetime—to know the Bible "by heart," to allow Scripture to have its way with your life. Your goal in reading Scripture is not only information. It is also formation. Set aside some time each day to read a portion of Scripture. Read a whole chapter, rather than just a few verses, if you can. Begin with a more coherent, straightforward narrative like the Gospel of Luke before you tackle something wild like Revelation. (One of our students calls Revelation "St. John on acid.")

Get a Good Bible Commentary

Be willing to be instructed by those commentators who have spent their whole lives interpreting Scripture. Using a Bible commentary is like sitting down and reading Scripture with a knowledgeable, wise friend. Be patient. Not every single passage on every day will speak to you. Keep at it. The Holy Spirit will enliven your reading if you just keep at the reading.

Expect to Change

God is not content to leave us as we are. In reading the Bible, we become God's promised new creations. God, the great

Creator, is not yet finished with the world or with your life. Don't risk reading the Bible if you are content with your life as it is. The Bible is busy creating a new world. John Calvin called Scripture the "lens" through which Christians view the world. As with a new pair of glasses, this new lens of the Bible brings into focus things we had not noticed before. Other things that once were special to us fade out of focus. Jesus was forever taking things that the world considered inconsequential—a widow's coin, a lost sheep, a lost boy—and forcing us to see these seemingly small and unimportant things as God sees them—as cherished, beloved creatures of the Creator. After you have heard from Jesus a story like that of the lost sheep, there is a good chance you will never again walk past some poor, lost, and wandering soul in the same way you once did. Jesus has given you a new "lens" for looking at the world. Over time, the Bible changes us by laying the story of God over our lives.

◈ PEOPLE OF THE BOOK ◈

The young man Jesus comes to his hometown synagogue in Nazareth (Luke 4). Perhaps it is "Student Recognition Sunday," when the students in the congregation are asked to help lead the service. Perhaps the congregation has heard that Jesus is thinking about attending seminary. At any rate, when Jesus returns, what do they do? They don't ask Him, "Tell us how it is for you in college." They don't say, "Share with us some of your personal spiritual experiences."

They do none of that. After all, these are Jews, people of the Book. Rather than asking Him to speak, they hand Jesus the Book, the scroll of the prophet Isaiah. He opens the scroll, and all are silent and attentive as He reads to them the ancient words of Scripture: "The Spirit of the Lord is upon me, because he has anointed me to bring good news to the poor."

When Jesus finishes reading, he begins to preach and interpret the passage, telling the congregation that these ancient words are being fulfilled among them that very day.

Admittedly, the congregation does not respond too favorably to His closing remarks. The Bible study ends that day with the congregation wanting to kill the teacher!

However, this incident reminds us that the Jews were people of the Book. And we are people of the Book, as well. We gather, submit to Scripture, listen, and align our lives accordingly. In such reading and hearing, God's Word has its way with us; we are being saved, being formed into God's people, being made disciples.

God's Word really is a lamp to our feet and a light to our path (Psalm 119:105).

DO I HAVE TO GO TO CHURCH TO BE A GOOD CHRISTIAN?

3 DO I HAVE TO GO TO CHURCH TO BE A GOOD CHRISTIAN?

Church bores me a lot of the time, and I think I can be just as good a Christian if I don't go. So what's the big deal?

We hear the question over and over again. There are so many people who find Jesus fascinating but want to know if going to church must be part of the deal of being a Christian. It's easy to understand where they're coming from, because in most instances, we've made the most dramatic movement in history dull. Whatever its ancient critics had to say about early Christianity, they never accused it of being boring. Back then, the Church stirred such emotions that some wanted to kill it, while others were ready to die to be a part of it. Jesus shocked people by turning water to wine (John 2). The Church dismays Jesus by turning his life-giving wine into tepid water! During its first century, nobody turned away from the Church because it was dull. Given what usually happens these days at the eleven o'clock hour on Sunday, it's obvious that we're going to have to make a strong case for getting new Christians involved in church. But that's exactly what we now intend to do.

✛ THE CHURCH FOR WHICH JESUS DIED ✛

The apostle Paul clearly declared that Jesus "loved the church and gave himself up for her" (Ephesians 5:25). The Church is called "the bride of Christ," and our Lord's affection for it went so deep that He was willing to die for it. Jesus' relationship with those in the Church was such that He deemed them more precious than the brothers and sisters with whom He had only biological ties. "Pointing to his disciples, he said, 'Here are my mother and my brothers! For whoever does the will of my Father in heaven is my brother and sister and mother'" (Matthew 12:49–50). To Jesus, the Church was His new family, and He prayed for its members to love each other as He and the one He called heavenly Father loved each other.

A Revolutionary Movement

To the apostle Paul, the Church was a people who were to be God's instrument for transforming the world (Romans 8:19ff). The Church, according to Paul, was to be a people destined to be a revolutionary movement that would ultimately invade all societal institutions and transform them into what God wanted them to be (Ephesians 1:22). This lofty view of the Church may seem hard to comprehend in today's world wherein the Church is so much a part of the dominant society that it is generally viewed as legitimizing the ruling establishment and sanctifying institutions. One critic called his Church "the Republican Party on its knees." It may seem hard to believe that the Church, which too often has supported racism, sexism, homophobia, and jingoistic national sin, originally was created to challenge the very principalities and powers that today are helping to sustain those evils.

To join the Church should be to join a movement committed to working with God to bring the gospel message to the world—and with it justice and well-being. The fact that the Church does not match its high calling is part of the challenge that faces new Christians. Part of each of their new faith commitments should be to make the Church that is into the kind of Church Paul declares that it should be.

The "New Israel"

The apostle Paul adds to our understanding of how important the Church is in the grand scheme of things when he treats the Church as the "new Israel." Paul viewed the Church as a new nation with a manifest destiny (Romans 11).

Paul had his reasons for referring to the Church as the new Israel. The old Israel, created through Abraham and Moses, was chosen to bring to the rest of the world God's vision of how society should be ordered, to be a "light to the nations" (Isaiah 42:6). But, according to Paul, when the old Israel considered its calling to be a privilege rather than a responsibility,

God called the new Israel (the Church) to take up the old Israel's mission. Thus, the Church was brought into existence, like the first Israel, to be a sign, a signal, a witness here on earth. But Paul warned that if the old Israel was cut off as God's special people because it failed to be and do what God required, God could likewise cut off the Church if it refused to live out its mission in the world (Romans 11:17–24).

The Body of Christ

Of all the things that the Bible says about the Church, none seems more important than when Paul refers to it as the "body of Christ" (1 Corinthians 12). Even to begin to understand this designation takes more than just a little explanation. But we will try. Christians believe that Christ, the second member of the Trinity, existed long before He became flesh as Jesus of Nazareth. According to Scripture, Christ was with the heavenly Father before the world was created (John 1:1–18). But the Bible goes on to declare that, two thousand years ago, this Christ took on human form and became incarnate in the historical person we know as Jesus of Nazareth who lived on this planet for about thirty-three years. In Christ, the fullness of Deity dwelt (Colossians 2:9); and

> **The Church was brought into existence to be a sign, a signal, a witness here on earth.**

through Him, we got a glimpse of what the character of God is really like (John 14:9). In and through Jesus, God touched people and healed them; He preached to them about His new Kingdom; He gave them hope; and most importantly, He loved them to the utmost.

The "Now" Body of Christ

Just as two thousand years ago Christ inhabited the body of Jesus through which to do His work in the world, so Christ inhabits a body in today's world for the same purpose. The Church is the Body of Christ, and when you and I become Christians, we become part of this body. For better or worse, this is the form the risen Christ has chosen to take in the world today.

Being declared part of the Body of Christ certainly elevates our humanity. It makes us, in biblical language, "heirs of God and joint heirs with Christ" (Romans 8:17). All that Christ once endeavored to be and do in the flesh, He now endeavors to do through us. The Spirit of Christ that was in Jesus is now alive in our mortal bodies (Roman 8:11). As wildly outrageous as it seems, we are declared to have the status of sons and daughters of God (John 1:12).

In practical terms, what all this means is that we, who are the "now" Body of Christ, are given the same mission that was given to the "then" body of Christ—which was Jesus. We are to preach, to teach, and to heal—even as Jesus did. We are to declare that the new social order He called "the kingdom of God" is at hand (Mark 1:15). We are to carry out Jesus' prophetic work, condemning injustices against the poor and calling for an end to all forms of oppression (Luke 4:18–19). For better or worse, we Christians, the Church, His Body, are the forms that the risen Christ has chosen to take in the world. What awesome faith Christ has in us!

Each Member—A Unique Function

The apostle Paul spells out the ramifications of our being collectively the "now" Body of Christ, even as Jesus was the "then" body of Christ. He analogously compares us with our diverse gifts and characteristics to being various parts of a human body. As the different parts of the human body have unique functions (e.g., the hands, the feet, the eyes), so the Body of Christ is made up of individuals, each of whom has a unique function. For instance, each of us has a special responsibility as part of the Body of Christ, according to the gifts God has given us (1 Corinthians 12:6–12). Some are gifted to be preachers, while others are gifted to heal people (and that includes doctors and nurses). Some are gifted to be teachers, while others are gifted to be prophetic voices within the Church. Paul says that each and every member of the Church has something special to contribute to the maintenance and building up of the rest of the Body. We are all called to use our gifts to help the Church be all it should be so that it can reach out to meet the needs of the world. (Ephesians 4:11–12).

Everybody is important in the Body of Christ. Paul makes that quite clear by pointing out that those who are hardly noticed and who might be deemed as nonessential often turn out to be the most necessary (1 Corinthians 12:20–24). This was illustrated clearly and humorously for Tony on a visit to a church in Indiana. Tony got to the church about an hour before the worship services were to begin. The door was open, so he went in. Wandering up and down the aisle of the church was an elderly man who looked up and gave him a friendly nod. Tony asked him if he was the church custodian, and he answered with a chuckle, "No way! I'm just exercising my gift of the Spirit."

"Which gift?"

"The gift of helps," he answered. "Check it out. It's in First Corinthians Twelve, verse twenty-eight. You'll find it there in black and white." Then he went on to say, "You know, this is one of those small churches that doesn't have a full-time preacher. The seminary down in Louisville always sends some student up here for weekends to do the preaching. Those kids come and go. The most any of them stay is a couple of years. Each one comes along with a real sense of importance, and they all do some good. But one of these days, old Charlie is gonna die," he said, referring to himself, "and then the people in this church will know who's really important. They'll really miss old Charlie with his gift of helps. The Sunday after I'm gone, they'll come to church, and they'll see that the grass wasn't cut and that nobody unlocked the doors for them to get in. The hymn books won't be in place, and the church bulletins won't be made up. If it's winter, maybe the snow won't be shoveled, and the heat won't be turned up. The way I figure, it'll be at least a month before they adjust to old Charlie's being gone."

Church is not a building or even a group of people. It's a happening!

He's right, of course. While at first glance old Charlie might not seem so important, careful notice will reveal that he is the heart and soul of that little church. He is the one who tells the visiting preachers who's in the hospital or who's having family troubles. He's the person who does the thousand and one things that need to be done to keep that little country church humming along. He is certainly a man with the gift of helps.

It must be noted that the Bible tells us that the gifts of the Spirit are given to the various members so that each can help, encourage, emotionally strengthen, and foster spiritual growth among the other members. These gifts are given to members so that the entire body of Christ might be able to effectively be God's change agent in the world. We are the body of Christ, created to do what Christ wants done for the world. Each of us must make it his or her duty to figure out what specific contribution we are to make to the rest of the body.

❖ MARKS OF THE CHURCH ❖

When it comes to understanding what the Church is supposed to be doing, theologians have come up with some Greek words to define its tasks. They are the *koinoniac* function, the *diakoniac* function, and the *kerygmatic* function.

Community

The *koinoniac* function is a Greek way of saying that church people are supposed to share a love for each other because they experience the presence of Christ in a special way. *Koinonia* means "community" or "fellowship." In the best sense, church is not a building or even a group of people. It's a happening! When Christian people interact in the kind of unique love that Jesus enables them to have for each other, something mystical happens. The Holy Spirit flows between them. The members sense themselves being knit together into a special fellowship called *koinonia*. Being a Christian, at its best, means that one feels as though he or she is caught up in some kind of collective ecstasy created by the Spirit of God.

A discernible sense of the Holy Spirit doesn't happen every time Christians get together, because as Jesus said,

"The wind blows where it chooses, and you hear the sound of it, but you do not know where it comes from or where it goes" (John 3:8). But there are special times when it does happen, and when it does, it reminds us of the day of Pentecost.

> When the day of Pentecost had come, they were all together in one place. And suddenly from heaven there came a sound like the rush of a violent wind, and it filled the entire house where they were sitting. Divided tongues, as of fire, appeared among them, and a tongue rested on each of them. All of them were filled with the Holy Spirit and began to speak in other languages, as the Spirit gave them ability. (Acts 2:1–4)

One exciting Sunday was recorded in an account by a pastor in Ann Arbor, Michigan. A young woman in the congregation had given birth to a child out of wedlock. She wanted her baby baptized, but there were no godparents to stand with her on the occasion. There was no family to be alongside her on her baby's special day. But when the pastor asked, "Who stands with this child to assure that he grows in the nurture and admonition of the Holy Spirit?" the whole congregation stood, as though on cue, and said, "We do!" They were, in that moment, a church—a church prompted by the Holy Spirit.

The Process *of Salvation*

There is often the illusion that "getting saved," as evangelists call it, is a one-time thing; but that's not true. The Bible makes it quite clear that, in reality, there is an ongoing *process* in getting saved. You were saved from the punishment of sin when you accepted Jesus as Lord and His death as a substitution for your own. But after you comprehended that truth, the process of being saved, or being transformed into the likeness of Jesus, just began. That process should go on and on until the old sinful life, as you have known it, has ended (Philippians 1:6). No one becomes so adept at being a disciple that he or she doesn't need, in a sense, to be caught up in an ongoing process of change. It is the responsibility of the Church to nurture this transformation of life. Through the mystical intimacy that is shared by Christians, you ought to be able to sense God's Spirit flowing into your life from others in your church, and the invasion of the Holy Spirit should further the ongoing change that is the salvation process. That's why we read in Acts 2:47 that "day by day the Lord added to their number those who were

> **Through the mystical intimacy that is shared by Christians, you ought to be able to sense God's Spirit flowing into your life from others in your church.**

being saved." No wonder the medieval church said that there is no salvation outside of the Church. As long as Church is defined not as a social institution but as "where two or three are gathered in [His] name" (Matthew 18:20), waiting for a sense of God's Spirit flowing in and through them to each other, I would say the same thing. There's just no way to become a Christian and stay solo.

Holy Communion

Of great importance is Holy Communion, the Lord's Supper, or the holy Eucharist. No matter how "low church" you get, when the Body of Christ assembles to eat the bread in remembrance of the broken body of Jesus on the cross and drink the wine in remembrance of His blood shed for the remission of sins, you are more than likely to sense that something sacred is happening. Leave it to the theologians to give confirming names to what is going on—names like transubstantiation and consubstantiation. But to every Christian, regardless of denominational affiliation, there is a sense that Christ is present in this time of worship in a way that is undeniably real. A hushed silence falls upon the congregation, even among exuberant Pentecostals, indicating that a mysterious blessing is being received. Being at the Lord's table in the Church does much to move you along toward the fullness of salvation. At the holy table, the people of the Church feel *koinonia* in a very special way.

Service

The second function of the Church is the *diakonic* function. In Greek, *diakonia* means "service" or "ministry." With this particular function, the Church takes upon itself the responsibility of serving people who are in need. The Church, at its best, can be counted on to be there for people who are suffering from poverty, sickness, and the sorrows of life's tragedies.

People Serving People

When the social system of this world (what the Bible calls the principalities and powers) grinds out human casualties, the people of God are supposed to rush in to pick them up, bind up their wounds, and wipe away their tears.

Individual Church members do a million and one things in living out the *diakonic* function. For instance, a friend of Tony's sits with a man dying of AIDS. He feeds him, and he carries him back and forth to sit on the toilet. He listens as the man voices his anger at all of those who turned their backs on him when they learned he was homosexual. Through it all, Tony's friend prays for the man and waits for him to reach out for God.

A church in New York City sends out members each night to be friends with the prostitutes on the street. They offer them hot coffee on cold nights, try to make sure the police do not abuse them, and do their best to provide them with medical care. They make no attempt to manipulate these women of the night into church; they simply serve them in the name of Christ.

A suburban Presbyterian church in Wayne, Pennsylvania, has organized scores of volunteers to go into Philadelphia, almost daily, to help out in a variety of urban ministries. They tutor at-risk children, they support programs for the homeless, and they make efforts to reach out to elderly city dwellers who often are afraid to leave their homes. Members of this church recognize that they are called by God to serve people in need.

The twin towers of the World Trade Center came tumbling down on September 11, 2001, and the Salvation Army was there ministering to people in shock, giving food and comfort to those at work looking for possible survivors, and providing counsel for the many who were trying to understand where God was to be found in the midst of this tragedy.

Working Change through the "System"

Many theologians claim that the Bible actually makes reference to social institutions. They say that when Paul uses the phrase "principalities and powers" in Ephesians 6, he is referring not only to demonic spirits but to all forces that exercise powerful influence on who we are and what we do. These forces, they say, include social institutions. Sociologists stress that much of who we are and what we do is controlled by the regulating effects of such institutions as the media, schools, business corporations, religious organizations, political systems, and role prescriptions. Paul admonishes us to realize that these principalities and powers can have destructive effects on all of us and that those destructive influences must be resisted. He tells us not to be conformed to these forces but to surrender to the transforming power of the Holy Spirit, who will help us combat them (Romans 12:2). In Ephesians 6:12, he writes: "For our struggle is not against enemies of blood and flesh, but against the rulers, against the authorities, against the cosmic powers of this present darkness, against the spiritual forces of evil in the heavenly places."

Members of this church recognize that they are called by God to serve people in need.

According to Paul, all of these principalities were willed into existence by God with the intention that they serve our needs and do good for society (Colossians 1:16). However, just as we as individuals have failed to be and do what our creator planned for us, so too have the principalities and powers become other than God intended them to be. Instead of doing good, they often generate all kinds of evil in society. Christians, in the face of such realities, are called to struggle to change the principalities and powers so that they might become instruments of God's blessings.

The good news is that, whatever shortcomings the Church may have, there are universal examples of the Church carrying out this *diakonic* mission: Hospitals have been established by the Church where there were none. The Church has built mission schools to give disadvantaged children a chance for a better life. And volunteers from the Church do many things from building houses for the poor with Habitat for Humanity to supporting holistic care for children in Third World countries through Compassion International.

Serving the poor and oppressed can eventually get the Church to recognize that ministering to the victims of a social system that lets people fall between the cracks is not enough. Those who get involved in the *diakonic* work soon realize that, for every hurting soul they lovingly patch up, the system turns out ten more to take his or her place. It doesn't take long to figure out that something has to be done to change the system itself so that it doesn't produce so many casualties.

Political conservatives claim that the way to change the system is to change people. They are convinced that, if individuals are impacted with the gospel message and converted, these converts will change the social system and make it more just and compassionate.

Political liberals, on the other hand, contend that people are messed up on the individualistic level because the social system has made them that way. Consequently, liberals tend to concentrate their efforts on changing the system itself, contending that messed-up people are the product of an evil social system.

In reality, both the conservatives and the liberals are partly right. The Church must preach a gospel that can have a transforming effect on individuals, while at the same time recognizing that the God who can save individuals from personal destruction wants to work through us to challenge the principalities and powers (biblical words for describing the social forces that condition human behavior) to become just and good. While we usually think of principalities and powers as demonic entities, many Bible scholars point out that they also may include social structures and other social forces that exercise influence on human behavior (see Hendrik Berkhof, *Christ and the Powers,* Herald Press). An example of this latter use is found in Romans 13 where Paul refers to "the powers" as the government. In short, we know that we cannot neglect either personal evangelism or the biblical call to transform society into a less oppressive and destructive system.

Rescuing people from pain and destruction requires that we work on both these fronts. And this leads me to explain the third function of the Church: the *kerygmatic* function.

Proclamation

In Greek, the word *kerygma* means "proclamation." This third function involves declaring to the world what God is doing in human history. The gospel the Church preaches does not minimize the significance of individualistic salvation at the expense of declaring what God wills to change in the social institutions that powerfully impact human behavior. It's not a matter of either/or. Instead, the gospel of the Church is both/and. As we get into discussing this third function of the Church, as defined by theologians, we need to keep that in mind.

The *kerygma* is the essence of the gospel message. In the *kerygmatic* function, the Church engages in putting into words the message that Jesus came to make known. In simple language, this means that the Church is called to evangelize the world.

People Telling People

The *kerygmatic* function requires that we tell as many people as possible about what Jesus did for them on the cross. Hearing the story of the death and resurrection of Jesus gives people the knowledge that is part of the salvation experience (Romans 10:14).

This messed up world in which we live has not been abandoned by God to the evil social forces.

Church people know that the Jesus who died for them has commissioned them to go into all the world and make this salvation story known to others. Realizing how the gospel story and the invasion of the Holy Spirit has impacted their own lives, true Christians should consider it an evil not to share the good news about Jesus with the rest of the world.

Imagine being given the cure to cancer and then keeping it to yourself. Would it not be evil to withhold the cure from the millions of suffering people who need it? Would you not be a despicable person if you saw people around you dying from cancer and remained unwilling to tell them what you knew? Knowing the cure to the guilt and anxieties that torture so many of the people around you, knowing the remedy for the meaninglessness of some of their lives, and knowing how to end the phobias about death that can drain the joy out of their living lays on you the responsibility of sharing what you know with those who need it so much.

Good News for the Entire World

But the *kerygmatic* function of the Church is more than just telling individuals what Jesus can do for them personally; it is also declaring the good news of what God is doing to and for the whole world. The God we worship is not just about helping individuals to subjectively experience the good feelings that go with being personally "saved." Our God is also at work on the societal level, changing institutions and even nations so that they might more fully embody justice and compassion. This messed-up world in which we live has not been abandoned by God to the evil social forces that seem to be everywhere evident. Instead, our God has entered human history in Jesus and has initiated a new social order that will one day completely replace the existence of the present flawed social order. Furthermore, our God maintains a physical presence in our world through the Church. It is God's purpose that, through those of us in the

Church, the social pathologies that plague our present world might be cured. In fulfilling its *kerygmatic* function, the Church declares that God's new regime is marked by the end of the exploitation of the poor, infant mortality, inadequate housing, gang violence, environmental destruction, neglect of the elderly, and a host of other social evils.

Unfortunately, the Church has been less than stellar in performing this particular part of its *kerygmatic* responsibility. One of the reasons is its fear of losing the support of some of its members who have a heavy investment in the present societal arrangement. Too often, we are more committed to our own various kingdoms than to the Kingdom of God. The Church has often backed away from taking strong, bold stands against social evils. Unlike the Bible prophets, there are leaders of the Church who regularly back off from doing anything that might disturb the ruling leaders of the established political-economic system.

For instance, instead of opposing oppressive dictators in such places as Latin American countries, church leaders have at times appeared on balconies with these tyrants, not too subtly endorsing their governments before the crowds below. Not long ago in South Africa, there were many church leaders who gave religious legitimacy to apartheid instead of condemning it. In our own country, there are church leaders who stand in the way of attempts to guarantee the constitutional rights of women, African-Americans, Hispanics, and gays.

Don't get the wrong idea. The Church's record isn't all bad. We have had our share of prophetic voices declaring that God's new social order is breaking loose in our world. Who can ignore the likes of Martin Luther King, Jr. and Bishop Oscar Romero, who became martyrs for the cause of God's justice? And how can anyone who wants to make a fair appraisal of the Church fail to notice Bishop Desmond Tutu, who risked every- thing for freedom in South Africa, and Dietrich Bonhoeffer, who abandoned the safety of an academic life in America to return to his native Germany and stand in opposition to Hitler, even though it cost him his life?

One of the most dramatic examples of a church leader who declared the love and justice of God's new regime against the dark and evil rulers of the old order can be found in Metropolitan Kyril, the fiery church leader in Plovdiv, Bulgaria's second-largest city, during World War II. When the S.S. troopers came to his city to round up the Jews, this head of the local Church stood against the Nazis and won a victory for the Kingdom of God. The S.S. troopers had gone so far as to gather the Jews together and herd them into a barbed wire enclosure. At the midnight hour, the Jews were to be pushed into cattle cars to be shipped to Auschwitz and death. Suddenly, at the end of the boulevard leading to the train sta- tion, Metropolitan Kyril appeared. He was a tall man to start with, and with his miter on his head he must have seemed like a giant as he led a large crowd of his church people toward the enclosure containing the captive Jews. The S.S. guards tried to stop him, but he laughed at them as he pushed aside their guns and climbed the gate to go in among the Jews. Metropolitan Kyril then recited one verse of Scripture and helped to change the destiny of a nation. From the Book of Ruth, he quoted this verse to the weeping and frantic captives who knew that death was just a few hours away: "Where you go, I will go; where you lodge, I will lodge; your people shall be my people, and your God my God" (Ruth 1:16). The Jews cheered him, as did the church people who had followed him to the train station. They were no longer Christians and Jews but a people united behind a prophetic leader of the Church. The S.S. troopers backed off, and the Jews were released. Not a single Bulgarian Jew died in a Nazi concentration camp, even though Bulgaria was one of the axis powers and an ally of Germany during World War II.

This is only one of a host of stories that evidences the words of Jesus when He said of the Church, "The gates of Hades will not prevail against it" (Matthew 16:18). When the Church declares the Kingdom of God in the power of the Holy Spirit, there are no walls of injustice or any doors to the citadels of evil that it cannot knock down.

❖ COME AS YOU ARE ❖

You may be saying to yourself, "All of these lofty words about the functions of the Church, as seen by theologians, do not cover up the reality that the Church has often failed miserably in carrying out these functions." It is hard to argue if you point an accusing finger at the Church and call it hypocritical. I'm not trying to be funny when I say, "That's why *you're* welcome to join." Christians are not a bunch of perfected saints waiting for you to become perfect before we let you join us. We'll accept you just as you are! The Church is a group of struggling Christians who, when honest, recognize their corporate hypocrisy even while continuing to try to make things right with their founder, Jesus Christ. You are welcome to join us because you are neither worse nor better than the rest of us. We all deserve to have Jesus turn His back on us because of our unfaithfulness, but the good news is that He doesn't. "For I am convinced that neither death, nor life, nor angels, nor rulers, nor things present, nor things to come, nor powers, nor height, nor depth, nor anything else in all creation, will be able to separate us from the love of God in Christ Jesus our Lord" (Romans 8:38–39).

St. Augustine once said, "The Church is a whore—but she's my mother." He recognized that as "the Bride of Christ," the Church has been unfaithful; and as "the Body of Christ," she has failed to effectively carry out her functions in the world. But at the same time, St. Augustine acknowledged that without the Church he never would have heard the gospel or experienced the loving care that nurtured him in his faith throughout his life. In spite of all of her weaknesses and shortcomings, St.

Augustine still acknowledged the Church as an essential part of the life of anyone who wants to be a Christian and to develop into a Christlike person. So in answer to the question, "Do I have to be a part of the Church to be a Christian?" the answer is "Yes!"

✢ WHICH CHURCH? ✢

Even if we convince you that going to church is a necessity for a Christian, you may still be perplexed and asking the question, "Which church?" There are all kinds of churches along the Christian spectrum, ranging from highly ritualistic congregations, as in Eastern Orthodox and Roman Catholic churches to free-wheeling, spontaneous Pentecostal congregations. What is even more confusing is that these highly varying congregations seem to have a hodgepodge of theologies and beliefs. "Which of them is the true Church?" you may ask, since many of them make the claim for themselves and some speak disparagingly about the others.

Finding Common Ground

Recognize that this problem is as old as Christianity itself; the apostle Paul wrote about it almost two thousand years ago. As Christianity moved from being a loosely knit movement into a worldwide organization, divisions quickly arose among believers. Paul writes:

Now I appeal to you, brothers and sisters, by the name of our Lord Jesus Christ, that all of you be in agreement and that there be no divisions among you, but that you be united in the same mind and the same purpose. For it has been reported to me by Chloe's people that there are quarrels among you, my brothers and sisters. What I mean is that each of you says, "I belong to Paul," or "I belong to Apollos," or "I belong to Cephas," or "I belong to Christ." Has Christ been divided? Was Paul crucified for you? Or were you baptized in the name of Paul? (1 Corinthians 1:10–13)

It is important to note that Paul addresses this problem by declaring that the important thing is that all Christians, regardless of their denominational labels, recognize that what they hold in common is an allegiance to Jesus Christ as Lord, Savior, and God. The World Council of Churches makes this its creed and contends that, in spite of differences that exist between members concerning forms of worship or secondary doctrines, all Christians are united around the primary doctrines of who Jesus is, what He did for us, and what we owe Him—obedience to His will in gratitude for our salvation.

Contemporary versus Traditional Worship Styles

There are some Christians, like Tony, who feel a spiritual kinship with those congregations that are into enthusiastic worship. While he will always love the worship services using the hymns with which he grew up, Tony has come to appreciate what is being called "contemporary worship." He relates positively to people praising God with uplifted hands, led by a worship team with guitars and drums. He is thrilled that this new kind of worship has a special attraction for young people and for many new converts whose experiences with Christ are marked by intense emotions. At Eastern College where Tony teaches, the students turn out in droves for chapel, even though chapel is voluntary. The primary attraction is the contemporary worship that goes on for twenty-five to thirty minutes before the speaker is introduced. Chapel has had to be moved into the gym in order to hold the crowds that come.

On the other hand, Tony's wife, Peggy, cringes whenever she finds herself in a contemporary worship setting. She jokingly says that the difference between contemporary worship music and a machine gun is that a machine gun only has a hundred rounds. The old hymns Peggy knows by heart are what speak best to her soul and create for her an atmosphere that fosters communion with God.

Will leads worship at Duke University in a great big neo-gothic, cathedral-like building with a big choir and *four* large pipe organs. It's all very traditional, very liturgical, but by any means not dull. Will loves the prayer and praise of the saints of the church past and in the church present.

There is room for all kinds of music and worship in God's kingdom. To paraphrase a passage of Scripture: "It's not this kind of worship or that kind of worship that matters. God is a spirit, and those who worship God must do so in spirit and truth." Furthermore, a close look at both praise music and the old hymns will demonstrate that each has some commendable virtues.

New converts, for the most part, seem to find themselves at home in the independent, newer churches and thrill to what they call the "real Christianity" that they find there. However, many of these people eventually transition to more traditional churches because they come to a place where sectarian Christianity doesn't speak to them anymore. Liturgical-type Christianity can also be very "real," especially to those who appreciate being connected to creeded traditions that are solid and secure. They enjoy the historic hymns that con-

> **There is room for all kinds of music and worship in God's kingdom.**

nect them with the saints of the past and give them assurances about the future. Many older people find a joy and comfort in singing the music they have memorized over the years.

In reality, most of us believe that there will be many kinds of worship in heaven. And, if that is the case, we ought to learn to be more affirming of churches that are different from our own here on earth. Join a church that allows you to be who you are before God and gives expression to the kind of worship that feels right for you, but try not to think your way is the only way. Remember what Paul teaches in Ephesians 4:4–6 when he writes: "There is one body and one Spirit, just as you were called to the one hope of your calling, one Lord, one faith, one baptism, one God and Father of all, who is above all and through all and in all."

Be ready to affirm that, as long as Christ is worshiped as Lord, Savior, and God, valid Christianity is being promoted—regardless of whether you are in an independent sectarian church or part of a mainline traditional congregation. If you want to be intimately related to Christ, you should want to be part of the community of believers that calls itself the "Bride of Christ." If you want to do Christ's work in the world, then you need to join up with Christians who are the "Body of Christ." And if you want to worship Christ in spirit and in truth, then you should be eager to join your voice with others who love Him and want to sing His praises.

It may sound strange to an outsider, but we believe that worship is the ultimate destiny of the Church. There are those who would make evangelism the thing that ultimately defines our raison d'etre. But the truth is that, in the end, evangelism is primarily recruiting people for a choir. Beyond time and history, evangelism will come to an end; but worship will never cease.

Then I heard what seemed to be the voice of a great multitude, like the sound of many waters and like the sounds of mighty thunderpeals, crying out, "Hallelujah! For the Lord our God the Almighty reigns. Let us rejoice and exult and give him the glory, for the marriage of the Lamb has come, and his bride has made herself ready; to her it has been granted to be clothed with fine linen, bright and pure"—for the fine linen is the righteous deeds of the saints. (Revelation 19:6–8)

AM I A SINNER?

4 AM I A SINNER?

There are these "Bible Thumpers" on our floor who keep telling me that I'm a sinner who has to get saved or else I'll go to hell. I know I'm not perfect, but I'm no worse than the next guy. To tell the truth, I think I'm a fairly decent person. Why do people like that go around labeling people like me in such a negative way?

First, a definition. Sin is not just something you did in the backseat of a Honda on a date in high school. Sin is whatever diminishes your humanness and/or diminishes the humanity of someone else. It's worse than just breaking some rules that were laid down before the foundation of the world. It's more dangerous than offending some transcendental Shylock who demands his pound of flesh from anyone who ticks him off. Sin is that which cuts into the heart of your being, tarnishes your dignity, dulls your capacity for ecstasy, and desensitizes you to any signals of love that others may send your way. Ernest Hemingway once said, "Sin is what you feel bad after doing." He was right, of course, but Hemingway never explained *why* you feel bad after doing it. We contend that the reason you feel bad after doing it is that it diminishes the essence of what makes you an actualized human being, the human being God created you to be.

Sin breaks God's heart. Because God is holy and can't stand sin, sin cuts us off from God. It alienates us from Him and leaves us with a sense of being estranged from what gives meaning and well-being to our lives.

✦ SIN CHEAPENS YOUR HUMANITY ✦

The expression "actualized human being" emerges from the psychology of Abraham Maslow. When asked to define the goal of existence, this dean of humanistic psychology answered that it was becoming a self-actualized human being. Such a person, he contended, would live in a state of total awareness of life, appreciating to the fullest its agonies and ecstasies. The self-actualized individual, according to Maslow, is one who has learned the gratification that comes from altruism and revels in the fulfillment derived from heroically giving oneself to that which enhances the well-being of others.

The reason we bring up the concepts of Abraham Maslow as we look for categories that define what it means to be human is that Maslow's description of what it means to be a self-actualized human being can be correlated easily with what the apostle Paul calls the qualities of spirituality. In Galatians 5:22–23 Paul writes: "The fruit of the Spirit is love, joy, peace, patience, kindness, generosity, faithfulness, gentleness, and self-control. There is no law against such things." Spirituality, according to

Paul, is living with one's eyes wide open to the mercies of God (Romans 12:1) and having ears that are able to absorb the revelations of the sacred in the midst of the mundane. Sin is what violates all of that.

If all of this rhetoric seems a bit esoteric, let's relate it to your own experiences. Have you ever been to a social gathering, perhaps a party, in which the talk and behavior were dehumanizing? We're talking about that time when you found yourself in conversation with people whose words and attitudes were such that on your way home, you had the sense that some of your goodness had been drained out of you and

Each time you fail to repent and find the spiritual strength to stand up and resist evil, you will be further along on your way to being desensitized.

that you yourself had been cheapened. Remember the time when you spent an evening in the company of people who made racist remarks, told sexist jokes, or verbally trampled all over those values you revere as sacred? Because you said nothing, you felt disgusted with yourself afterward. You realized that you had lost some of your dignity as a human being, and you had a sick feeling in the pit of your stomach.

What we're trying to say is that sin does that to you, and each time you fail to repent and find the spiritual strength to stand up and resist evil, you will be further along on your way to being desensitized. After a certain number of such moral failures, you will probably learn to be comfortable in such dehumanizing settings.

All sin cheapens your humanity. Lying may seem like "a very present help in time of trouble," but it dissipates your self-respect. Adultery has an adventuresome thrill to it in the beginning, but the sneaking, deception, and betrayal of trust that adultery involves create shame. Even if it is undiscovered, adultery eats away at the intimacy you had with the partner whose love you once enjoyed. Novelist Graham Greene said that sin renders us "burnt-out cases," incapable of experiencing the thrills that should go with sex.

Murder has to be the ultimate attack on the humanity of another, but it is also an act that leaves the murderer with a deadened soul. In the movie *Crimes and Misdemeanors,* Woody Allen goes to a cocktail party where he finds himself alone with a doctor who confesses that he has silenced the lover who threatened to expose him by having his brother kill her. The doctor describes how, at first, he was tortured day and night by the terrible immensity of what he had done but that after a while, he learned to live with it. He explains that eventually he came to a place where he hardly thought about it at all, and when he did, it bothered him only mildly. The doctor doesn't realize that, when he took the life of another, something precious was taken from his own soul and he was left with an indifference that, like cancer, silently eats away at all that makes for vital living.

On a subconscious level, sin destroys your ability to live life in the "now" with full intensity. Repressed guilt and the fear of being found out dissipate your psychic energy into that which is past. Unconscious anxieties about the possible consequences of what you have done distract the vital attention you should be giving to the present. But if your energies and focus are being consumed by the past and future, you haven't much left to concentrate on life in the here and now. Thus, the consequences of sin are not only some possible punishment in the next life: They are the loss of the capacity to experience the fullness of life in the present.

There are those who contend that sinning is only human. In reality, sin is just the opposite. Sin diminishes what lies at the core of being human.

✧ GOD'S LAW ENABLES YOU ✧ TO BE FULLY HUMAN

In the beginning, our original parents, Adam and Eve, were created to be in the image of God. That's what God intended for them. But they sinned and that image was marred, and they lost a good bit of their humanness. The good news is that Jesus came to undo the effects of sin. He is among us *now*, and His purpose is not only to give us a heavenly life after death but also to restore the humanness we lost because of sin. Thus Paul writes:

"For as all die in Adam, so all will be made alive in Christ. But each in his own order: Christ the first fruits, then at his coming those who belong to Christ" (1 Corinthians 15:22–23).

We've gone through this explanation of sin to overcome the simplistic idea that once upon a time God arbitrarily drew up a set of rules and that those who break them will be punished by God, who is, in the end, a celestial hanging judge. This is not to say that God is not a lawgiver or that God is not a punisher of evil who demands justice. What we're saying is that the God of Scripture loves us enough to lay down rules that are guidelines to help us become as fully human as possible and thus reflect the image of our Creator. God wants to have a loving, interactive friendship with us, and that fellowship is not possible unless we actualize our humanity. The rules in the Bible are directives to guide us into humanizing actions and humanizing relationships with each other.

> **The God of Scripture loves us enough to lay down rules that are guidelines to help us reflect the image of our Creator.**

The ancient rabbis studied the laws of God and pleaded with their people to obey them, not because they were concerned about punishments and rewards in the next life, but because they viewed the laws of God as instructive for becoming the glorious people we were intended to be while in *this* life—that is, fully actualized human beings. Jews see the law of God not as restrictive rules but as the gracious gift of a God who loves us enough to show us the way to abundant life. As you read through the Hebrew Bible, you will find almost nothing about life after death, and some of the most orthodox Jews, both then and now, make little reference to the afterlife. Many Jews think that the afterlife may not exist at all (Matthew 22:23–33). These orthodox Jews believe that the benefits of living according to the lifestyle prescribed by the laws of Scripture enable us to realize our potential as creations destined to be conformed to the image of God.

We Christians believe the same thing, even though we believe that the completeness of our humanity will not be accomplished in this life—that is what heaven is for. There, according to the old Wesleyan hymn, "we shall be what we would be"; our humanity will be fully actualized. The image of God in us, lost in the Fall of humanity because of sin, will be fully restored, and we will become like the second Adam—Jesus— who called Himself "the Son of Man" (John 8:28). "Son of Man" suggests that Jesus, being the incarnation of God, shows us what it is like to be fully human.

❖ LEGALISM DEGRADES YOUR HUMANITY ❖

Watch out for legalism! There are those who forget what the laws of God were meant to achieve and try to use them to degrade the very humanness that God intended for us. They do this by adding to the laws of God their own interpretations and meanings, and in so doing, they turn what was intended to help us live life at its most abundant and fulfilling level, into an array of stultifying, trivial regulations that burden us down and sap our joy. Legalists thus turn the good news of God's love for us into the bad news of a moralistic scheme for saving ourselves all by ourselves.

Jesus had to deal with legalists in His day. Once, when He tried to heal a man on the Sabbath day, He was extremely troubled by them. "Again he entered the synagogue, and a man was there who had a withered hand. They watched him to see whether he would cure him on the sabbath, so that they might accuse him. And he said to the man who had the withered hand, 'Come forward' " (Mark 3:1–3).

Obviously, these legalists viewed obedience to the laws of God, *as they defined them,* as an end in itself, rather than as a means to an end.

As you make the Christian journey, you will encounter those who not only lay down rules and regulations that they themselves invented but also act as though their legalisms are ordained by God. For instance, when Tony was a kid, the Baptist church to which he belonged took a dim view of dancing. Some of the church folk said that those who were into such activities were into sin. We are hard pressed to find anything in the Bible that supports such beliefs. Many in the evangelical circles in which Tony travels believe that having a glass of wine is a sin, yet when he was in Argentina, Tony found that some of the most fundamentalist Christians had wine with just about every meal.

How Paul Dealt with Legalism

Sometimes we need to obey the legalisms of a particular group for no other reason than that taking a stand against its rules would create more upset than it's worth. How the apostle Paul dealt with eating meat that had been offered to idols provides one set of guidelines for us today. It seems that in certain Greek cities, pagan religious worshipers would offer high quality meat to their gods. Since their gods were nothing more than stone and metal idols, the meat was left untouched. It was then taken and sold at bargain prices by the temple priests, who made a good living off of such transactions. Many Christians saw this meat as a good deal and were more than ready to buy it. There were, however, other Christians who contended that buying this meat was sinful because it was financially supporting pagan religions and that since the meat had been offered to idols, even eating the meat was a form of idolatry. Paul blew off the legalistic opinions of those who condemned the practice of buying and eating this meat. However, he went on to say that if the practice of Christians eating this meat became a major stumbling block to those legalists, whom he called "weaker brothers," and kept them from fellowship with other

Christians and so preoccupied them that they could not deal with the deeper concerns of faith, then he would be more than willing to give up the practice. He writes:

> Hence, as to the eating of food offered to idols, we know that "no idol in the world really exists," and that "there is no God but one." Indeed, even though there may be so-called gods in heaven or on earth—as in fact there are many gods and many lords—yet for us there is one God, the Father, from whom are all things and for whom we exist, and one Lord, Jesus Christ, through whom are all things and through whom we exist.
>
> It is not everyone, however, who has this knowledge. Since some have become so accustomed to idols until now, they still think of the food they eat as food offered to an idol; and their conscience, being weak, is defiled.... Therefore, if food is a cause of their falling, I will never eat meat, so that I may not cause one of them to fall. (1 Corinthians 8:4–7, 13)

Even though legalism was a pain in the neck to Paul, he was willing to put up with it—to a point. But when legalism hurt people by destroying Christian fellowship or keeping them from Jesus, Paul declared war on those who promoted it. For instance, when Peter went along with some legalistic practices of Judaism, which would have made Gentiles second-class citizens in the Church, Paul went ballistic and said, in effect, "enough is enough, already!" (Galatians 2:11ff).

A Legalistic View of Temptation

One example of legalists going by the letter of the law and putting a burdensome guilt trip on people is in the matter of dealing with temptation. They point out that Jesus seemed to suggest that even to have the desire to commit sin cross your mind makes you just as guilty of committing the sin as if you had actually done it. They cite Jesus as saying: "You have heard that it was said, 'You shall not commit adultery.' But I say to you that everyone who looks at a woman with lust has already committed adultery with her in his heart" (Matthew 5:27–28). Going by the letter of the law, rather than by the spirit, when it comes to this particular scriptural passage, Jesus Himself would be made a sinner. After all, the Bible tells us that Jesus was tempted in every way as we are tempted: "For we do not have a high priest who is unable to sympathize with our weaknesses, but we have one who in every respect has been tested as we are, yet without sin" (Hebrews 4:15). According to legalists, just being tempted is

When legalism hurt people, Paul declared war on those who promoted it.

to have sinned, and that, by their definition, would have made Jesus a sinner. Yet that same verse declares that He was without sin.

Getting into the spirit of what Jesus is really talking about in Matthew 5:27–28, we realize that any thoughts that preoccupy us in a way that allows us to hurt others, such as by treating them as sexual objects, are sinful. When Jesus said that you don't have to kill a person to destroy that person, He implied that diminishing the dignity of another and subtracting from that person's humanity by the way you talk is a kind of murder. "You have heard that it was said to those of ancient times, 'You shall not murder'; and 'whoever murders shall be liable to judgment.' But I say to you that if you are angry with a brother or sister, you will be liable to judgment; and if you insult a brother or sister, you will be liable to the council; and if you say, 'You fool,' you will be liable to the hell of fire" (Matthew 5:21–22).

When what goes on in one person's mind translates into attitudes that regard others as less than human, that is sin. Racist, sexist, and homophobic attitudes are sin because they do horrible things to other people—even if those others are not physically harmed.

Sin has a way of sending you into a nosedive. The more you do it, the easier it is; and the dehumanization that goes with it progresses in ways you hardly notice. Progressively, you grow further away from God and from the true self God created you to be. It may be that sooner or later you will get a wake-up call that shakes you into an awareness of what is happening. There may be a sickness or an accident that threatens your future. Or perhaps you get into trouble over your head. Maybe you hear a sermon that brings you under conviction, or perhaps somebody you care about forces you to take a good look at yourself. We can't tell you when or how, but we're pretty sure you will have a crisis moment in which you come face to face with a strong desire to change. Christians call that repentance!

✧ REPENTANCE BRINGS RENEWAL AND ✧ TRANSFORMATION

Repentance is *not* just saying you're sorry. It's even more than going on to say that you are not going to repeat your mistakes of the past. True repentance involves a whole turnaround in your life in which you commit yourself to becoming what you were meant to become when God created you. In the gospels, the Greek word for "repentance" is *metanoia*, the same root word for our "metamorphosis." To repent is to experience a metamorphosis. Repentance is being transformed into whom God created you to be—just like a butterfly emerges from a cocoon. It's turning away from behavior and attitudes that have been dehumanizing you and hurting people around you and undergoing a process of renewal. This renewal is a recovering, little by little, of the humanness that you've lost because of sin. It involves getting into right relationships with God and with others. It requires spending time alone in prayerful meditation, pouring your heart out to God, begging for forgiveness, and yielding to a sense of forgiveness that you can only receive from God in the context of stillness. In some cases—when doing so will not cause further suffering and pain—it requires confessing your sin to those whom you have hurt, as hard as that may be. You also need to go off by yourself and confess your sin to God. Out of such confession, a healing process begins: "If we confess our sins, he who is faithful and just will forgive us our sins and cleanse us from all unrighteousness" (1 John 1:9).

If it's going to work, true repentance requires that you face up to your weaknesses and recognize that, without help from God, you'll probably end up back in your old sinful ways. This is where the Holy Spirit comes in. You need to pray that the Holy Spirit invades you and enables you to be better than you could be on your own. The Bible promises that God will be there for you when you call out for help. Philippians 2:13 says, "For it is God who is at work in you, enabling you both to will and to work for his good pleasure."

Consistently overcoming the inclination to sin requires sharing your need for help with close Christian friends. This is essential because, as it says in Galatians 6:2, fellow Christians helping each other out and bearing one another's spiritual burdens provide the support system you need to "fulfill the law of Christ." With prayer and with fellow Christians holding you accountable, there is no temptation that will be too great for you to handle. Again, you have the promise of Scripture: "No test-ing has overtaken you that is not common to everyone. God is faithful, and he will not let you be tested beyond your strength, but with the testing he will also provide the way out so that you may be able to endure it" (1 Corinthians 10:13).

Repentance for Corporate Sin

There's one kind of sin that's very hard to discern and sel-dom creates the kind of guilt that will drive you to repentance. It's corporate sin. We're talking about the kind of sin that results from those power interests and social institutions that dehu-manize others. In the world in which we live, there are things we do collectively, rather than individually, that oppress people. The principalities and powers, because they are large, impersonal, and corporate, delude us into thinking that we have no responsibility for what they do.

Just the other day, Will put on a sports shirt and happened to notice the label: "Made in Honduras." More than likely, that shirt was made by poorly paid child laborers. We profit from the suffering of others by wearing such clothes. Is this sin?

Recently, Tony became involved in trying to address some of the problems of public education in the school system of Philadelphia. He learned that students who live within the city limits get $1,900 less per year spent on them than do students who live in any of the suburban townships. Extrapolated, that means that a class of thirty in the city has $57,000 less per year spent for its education than does a class of thirty in any of the school districts outside the city. Such inequities leave urban children with outdated textbooks, dilapidated school buildings, and classes that are too large for good teaching. Things like computers become scarce luxuries. No single individual is responsible for creating such inequities, and few are even aware of what's going on. Instead, social policies such as funding education with real estate taxes are to blame. In Philadelphia, huge amounts of real estate are tax exempt because they are used for such things as university campuses, churches, parks, and museums. The remaining property that is still taxable often has old and rundown buildings on it and such a low market value that it yields little tax revenue. Contrariwise, suburban school districts are often comprised of high-priced real estate and, therefore, can collect huge revenues from taxes.

Corporate sin that results in structural evil has to be exposed.

Although the world refers to such inequality as "the challenge of education finance," this kind of unjust arrangement should be called "structural evil." The ways in which things have been set up by the laws and economic arrangements of various communities leads to urban children being short changed. As a result, many of them fail to realize their God-given potential. Such sin is not the result of what people do individually; it comes from the way those in positions of power have structured the financing of schools.

Corporate sin that results in structural evil has to be exposed before the general public can even begin to feel any guilt about it or be driven to any acts of repentance. It is your Christian obligation to learn as much as you can about how businesses, media, government, and other social systems sometimes function oppressively so that you can work for social justice and endeavor to set things right. Sin is sin; it is dehumanizing rebellion against the purposes of God, whether it occurs in a bedroom or a boardroom.

Repentance for corporate sin requires collective action and as a Christian, you are required to do what you can to change things. Social systems that dehumanize the poor (and the poor are usually the victims) must be challenged in the name of Jesus and aided in metamorphosis. Environmental degradation, the debts of Third World countries that leave the poorest of the poor to pay for the failures of their governments, the trade arrangements that cause weak nations to be exploited unfairly by the business interests of strong nations, and the discrimination minority groups must often endure when trying to get jobs are just some of the corporate sins that come from structural evil. Sins on the societal level seldom generate personal feelings of guilt, despite their dehumanizing consequences. Nevertheless, we need to repent of them and take the political action that is essential to make things right.

We have spent much time talking about our corporate sin because, in our experience, that's the sin that is most difficult for many of us to recognize. Sometimes it's easier to be honest about our personal faults than to see the faults in our nation. Yet whether personal or corporate, sin tends to be of one piece.

Returning to Your Best Self

Sin is not only rebellion against God's will for us, but it is also rebellion against our own best selves, the humanity that God has intended for us. Therefore, when we repent, when we turn around and turn back toward God, when we let go of our sin and embrace new life in Jesus, we are also returning to our best selves.

You can see this turning in Jesus' great story of the Prodigal Son (Luke 15). The younger son said, in effect, "Dad, drop dead!" Put the will into effect; give me my inheritance now! And the father did just that. He gave the young man (whom we estimate to be about the age of a college sophomore) his share. The boy took it and went out into the "far country," where Jesus says he indulged in some "wild living." When all the money was gone, and he was hungry and in rags, the boy hit bottom. Right then, in Jesus' wonderful phrase, "he came to himself." We like that. He came to himself. He came back to his real self. He said, in effect, "Here I am out here living like a pig when I've got a father. I've got a home."

It was the beginning of his great turning, his homecoming,

his turning back, not only to the father but to his own true self as he was created to be. That's repentance.

We must be honest in admitting that Jesus tended to talk a great deal more about forgiveness than He did about sin. Perhaps He talked so much about forgiveness because He knew that it is almost easier to convince us that we are sinful—that is, weak, rebellious, stubborn, stupid, lustful, addicted, and all the rest—than it is to convince us that God loves sinners! The reason we spend so much time talking about sin is to remind ourselves that Jesus Christ came to save sinners. Only sinners.

We are all sinners, both on the personal and on the corporate societal levels. However, we are not simply to resign ourselves to this reality, shrug our shoulders, and act as though things cannot be changed. Jesus comes to each of us and offers to help us turn things around so that we can press toward right-

Sin is not only rebellion against God's will for us, but it is also rebellion against our own best selves.

eousness, so that we can work until justice rolls down upon our world like a mighty stream and we are fully restored to all God created us to be—beloved, loving children of a loving God.

HOW DO I KNOW WHAT'S RIGHT?

5

HOW DO I KNOW WHAT'S RIGHT?

We are faced today with so many difficult issues—
abortion, euthanasia, drugs. What can an ancient
book like the Bible have to say about these really
tough ethical issues? I've always believed that being
a Christian is mostly a matter of doing what's right
and behaving the way God wants. But with all the
different viewpoints out there, how can a Christian
know what's right?

A fellow student comes up to you at a party, gives you a
knowing look, shoves a tiny tablet in your hand, smiles, and
says, "Here, take this. You'll feel good all over."

The housing director on campus tells you that the room
assignments have been made for next fall and that she has
assigned you a roommate who is "a really great girl." "But,"
she says, "it's only fair for me to tell you that she is a different
race from you. I hope that's no problem." Is it a problem?

On your way to a movie last Saturday, walking down the
street with friends, this dirty looking, unshaven man came up
to you and said, "I'm not lying. I'm hungry, and I need some
money. Will you give me a couple of dollars for a meal?
Please?"

Well, you're a Christian. Will your faith commitments make
any difference in the way that you decide what you ought to

do in these cases? We have said earlier that Christians are big on the Bible. Does the Bible offer any clear directives on ethical dilemmas such as these?

You are growing up in an age of moral relativity. In your sociology courses you have learned that there can be great diversity between how one culture defines right and wrong and how another culture defines it.

"The world isn't done in black and white," says your philosophy professor. "There are a few sharp lines between right and wrong, but it's mostly a matter of personal preference or who has power in a given society."

In such a world, being a Christian—a person who believes in something called "God's will" or the "Ten Commandments" or "right and wrong"—sometimes feels like being a member of a minority. As we have admitted earlier, to be a Christian is to be a member of a counterculture, to have an alternative to the world's way of doing things. What makes Christian ethics Christian? When a Christian is confronted with an ethical dilemma, do we bring anything to the problem that is different from that which any other caring, moral person might bring?

✧ CHRISTIANITY IS ABOUT RELATIONSHIP ✧

A friend says to you, "Well, I don't go to church, and I'm not all that *religious*, but I do believe in God, and I try to do the right thing and be kind to others. After all, that's what Christianity is all about, right?"

Wrong.

Being a Christian is not primarily a matter of believing a set of propositions about God or about behaving within certain guidelines. Beliefs are important in this faith, but Christianity is more than a philosophy of life. Doing the right thing is essential, but the Christian faith is more than a matter of vaguely being kind to others or even following a set of rules. Christians do have rules, but before this faith is about rules, it is about *relationship*. Christianity is about relationship with Jesus Christ and letting that relationship influence all our lives. Christians are those who are friends with God.

Doing the right thing is essential, but the Christian faith is more than a matter of following a set of rules.

Certainly many people do good, even people who do not worship Jesus. But when Christians worship God and do good deeds, we do it because of our relationship with Christ. In Sunday worship, for example, when we give of our money and sing songs of worship, it is as if we are laying our lives before God, offering ourselves up in praise to Him. When Christians worship God, love the poor, do not take advantage of others, or stand up for what's right, they do it not out of fear of punishment or in order to keep their slates clear or out of an attempt to look better than everyone else. Christians do it all for love— the very best motivation of all.

105

Christians attempt to do good and live godly lives as a loving response to the God who first loved us. "We love because he first loved us" (1 John 4:19). Christian ethics is our way of loving the God who, in Christ, has loved us. We are to love God with all our heart, soul, and strength (Deuteronomy 6:5)—in other words, with everything we've got.

After Israel's great exodus from slavery, God spoke to the people He had delivered: "So now, O Israel, what does the LORD your God require of you? Only to fear the LORD your God, to walk in all his ways, to love him, to serve the LORD your God with all your heart and with all your soul, and to keep the commandments of the LORD your God and his decrees that I am commanding you today, for your own well-being" (Deuteronomy10:12–13).

Yet how, specifically, are we to obey the requirements to walk in God's ways, to love and to serve God with "all your heart and with all your soul"?

❖ FIVE ANSWERS TO "WHAT'S RIGHT?" ❖

As we see it, there are at least five major ways Christians have answered the question "How do I know what's right?"

1. Follow the Rules

When confronted with some ethical dilemma, many Christians say that it's simple, just follow the rules. God has graciously given us His will for the world. The Bible contains many directives, prohibitions, admonitions, and laws. Just follow the rules.

The Old Testament repeatedly speaks of the Law of God, the Torah, as a gift. God has not left us to wander about aimlessly, having to discover for ourselves which path to take and which to avoid. One set of guidelines He's given us is the Ten Commandments (Exodus 20:1–17). David, in the Book of Psalms, praises God's law: "The law of the LORD is perfect, reviving the soul; the decrees of the LORD are sure, making wise the simple" (Psalm 19:7).

The laws within Scripture prescribe an orderly, dependable world where actions have consequences. But our culture tends to look at law as an abridgement of our freedom. We don't like anyone telling us what to do. We think of law as prohibitive, restrictive. Israel, on the other hand, believed that the law of God was a gift of God that made truly human life possible. G. K. Chesterton once said that if you walk to the edge of a cliff and keep walking, you will not break the law of gravity; you will prove it! Many people today are not so much breaking the laws of God, they are also demonstrating, in the sad results of their disordered lives, the validity of God's laws.

Jesus, good Jew that He was, loved and studied the Law. "Do not think that I have come to abolish the law or the prophets" (Matthew 5:17), He told His disciples. He often intensified rather than relaxed the requirements of the Old Testament law, frequently saying, "You have heard it said of old…but I say to you…" Though the Law of Moses permitted a man to divorce his wife, Jesus condemned divorce in the strongest terms, possibly because the older laws of divorce gave all the rights to men and none to women.

Laws can tell people what is right and what is wrong, but laws alone cannot make people *do* what is right.

Yet it is also true that Jesus was criticized by the religious authorities for not keeping the sabbath. He mocked those who had pride in their own success at keeping the law rather than in God. He criticized some of the religious leaders of His day who worried about inhaling a gnat and ended up "swallow[ing] a camel"! (Matthew 23:24).

Jesus taught that, while the laws of Scripture were helpful and good, more than obedience to the law was required in order to foster the "higher" righteousness that God's kingdom demands.

The apostle Paul said that all who rely on the law are under a "curse," because "a person is justified not by the works of the law but through faith in Jesus Christ" (Galatians 2:16). Paul believed that Jesus, while not abrogating the law, had replaced the law as the major means of relating us to God. Our relationship with God is not dependent upon our moral perfection and goodness, for who among us, no matter how hard we try, is perfect and sinless? Our relationship to God is totally dependent upon God's goodness in Christ. In Jesus, "Apart from the law, the righteousness of God has been disclosed.… For there is no distinction; since all have sinned and fall short of the glory of God; they are justified by his grace as a gift" (Romans 3:21, 22b–24a).

We are related to God, not through anything that we do, but because of something that He did for us in Christ. Our relationship with Him is a *gift,* and we have a word for this gift: *grace.*

Let's be honest. Laws have their limits. Laws can tell people what is right and what is wrong, but laws alone cannot make people *do* what is right. Righteousness requires inner motivation. Furthermore, merely following the law does not go far enough. There is a big difference between merely avoiding evil and actively doing good. There are even some extreme situations in which a person might be forced to break the law in order to do good.

Most laws are best seen as principles for behavior, guides for doing good, rather than hard-and-fast rules for all situations. Sometimes we must make decisions not only on the basis of the law but also on the basis of our assessment of the possible results of our actions. "Love does no wrong to a neighbor; therefore, love is the fulfilling of the law" (Romans 13:10).

2. Follow the Gang

To tell the truth, most of us give little thought to what we do. We simply follow the crowd. We rarely stop and ask,

"What does the Bible say?" or even, "What would Jesus do?" We say, "Well, everybody else is doing it." You know how powerful peer pressure can be. We want to fit in, to be popular. So we justify what we do by saying, "Everybody on this campus" cheats on exams, gets drunk on weekends, has casual sex, lies. "Everybody" becomes our god.

As Christians, we must remember that it was the crowd of "everybody" that, when confronted with Jesus, cried, "Crucify Him!" Righteousness is not a matter of majority vote. The greatest heroes of the contemporary church—Bonhoeffer, who was martyred by the Nazis; Martin Luther King, Jr., who fought for racial justice; Dorothy Day, who worked with the poor in the slums—are those who dared, out of love for Christ and His kingdom, to brave the mob, go against the flow, and swim against the stream. As Malcolm Muggeridge said, "Only dead fish swim with the stream."

There are times when Christians must be like the first apostles and stand up against the crowd and declare, "We must obey God rather than any human authority" (Acts 5:29b).

One day President Lincoln asked a committee that was mired in protracted discussion, "How many legs would a sheep have if you called it's tail a leg?" They thought and replied, "Five." Lincoln retorted, "No, it would only have four, because calling a tail a leg does not make it one."

3. Obey Your Conscience

Some people think of morality as mostly a matter of intuition. "I know what is right or wrong. It's that little voice inside me. I let my conscience be my guide," they say. Who dares to challenge anyone who says, "I sincerely believe that what I did was the right thing to do. Who are you to question me?" There is, they believe, no right or wrong if what we do is "sincerely" what we think we ought to do.

But in matters of Christian ethics, sometimes sincerity has nothing to do with it. Misguided people have done some terrible, horrible things, all the while sincerely believing that what they did was right. Sometimes a person can say, "My conscience is clear," because his or her head is empty!

With conscience, the old "garbage in, garbage out" applies. If a person has been trained in the disciplines of honesty, humility, self-examination, forgiveness, and all the other virtues that go into truly Christian morality, then that person's appeal to "conscience" is worthwhile. However, for too many people, the appeal to conscience or sincerity is a cop-out—a way of keeping their morality safe from critical scrutiny. Most of our consciences are products of our backgrounds, the way we have been brought up. Most of us tend to believe something is right simply because that's what we've always been told was right. Conscience alone is not a sufficient guide to right and wrong.

4. Let the Situation Be Your Guide

Some Christians are suspicious of rules, principles, and hard-and-fast laws for ethical behavior. They know that Jesus rarely engaged in ethical deliberation but rather reached out in love to specific people in specific situations. They point out that sometimes Jesus risked the disapproval of the religious authorities in order to embrace someone whom the rules of the day labeled untouchable. These people say that Jesus abided by only one law—the law of love. They maintain that the end justifies the means and that the end of all Christian action ought to be love. They believe that we must courageously and creatively respond to each situation in life with loving action, regardless of the rules. Some have called this approach "situation ethics."

Stealing, lying, and the taking of life are all condemned by the Bible and Christian tradition. Is there ever any situation in which stealing, lying, or killing might be justified on the basis of love? A student becomes pregnant. While she feels that abortion is wrong, she asks herself, "Is it fair to bring a child into the world when I don't really want a baby and don't feel that I have the maturity to raise a baby?" Furthermore, she asks herself, "Should I cause my parents this embarrassment?" She therefore concludes that the most "loving" thing to do for herself, her unborn child, and her parents is to have an abortion.

This instance shows some of the weaknesses in the "love is

all you need" argument. Do we really have the maturity, self-honesty, and goodness to make such decisions? It is so easy to rationalize our behavior in the name of some vague, mushy thing called "love." Is some ephemeral inclination called "love" enough to guide us through moral quandaries?

Sometimes, when you are dating, you learn the hard way that when someone says to you, "I love you," what he or she may really mean is, "I love me, and I want to use you to love me even more."

Besides, it is not true that every situation is unique and utterly original. Christians are able to benefit from the examples of those who have gone before us, profiting from the guidance and counsel of those saints who have preceded us in the faith. It is arrogant for people in any generation to assume that they are the first generation on the face of the earth to struggle with issues of greed, lust, and carnal desire. Christians are not to act in lonely isolation or to say, "My situation is so special, so unique, that those who have gone before me in the faith have nothing to contribute to my ethical deliberation. I am therefore going to decide for myself on the basis of what I believe 'love' to be in this situation."

Christians must make decisions in community, relying on the combined wisdom of the church, saints who died long ago, and on our fellow Christians living today. This community of faith and experience guides us, helps us critique our situation, and offers us counsel and advice.

5. Live in Relationship with Christ

Whatever else it means to be a Christian, it means to be someone who is becoming friends with Christ. Your generation, in our experience, puts a high value on relationships and friendships. We believe that may be one of your strongest assets in developing your discipleship.

Nowhere does Jesus say that the commandments or the rules of Scripture are irrelevant. Yet He sharply criticizes those who believe that, because they have obeyed the Law, they are more righteous than anyone else. He condemns those who think morality is only a matter of keeping one's personal slate clean, just refraining from doing wrong. For Jesus, ethics is also a matter of courageously and intentionally doing good, that is, trying to conform your life to the shape of the Kingdom of God.

> **Nowhere does Jesus say that the commandments or the rules of Scripture are irrelevant.**

Jesus believed that the law was good but that it did not go far enough. Goodness comes through being in love with Jesus and living in a trusting, obedient relationship with God. Then we will love others in the same compassionate, forgiving, actively seeking way that we have been loved by God through Christ. Christians do good, live courageously, stand up for what is right, and reach out to the suffering—but not because we are trying thereby to get in God's good graces.

Think of it this way. Your parents want you to do well in college, so what if, the night before you leave home for college, they were to sit you down and say, "Now look, we have made lots of sacrifices for you. We have spent a fortune on your education. Therefore, you owe us something. We need you to go to college and work hard and make great grades. If you don't, we might not receive you back home for the Christmas holidays. We might even disinherit you if your grades are an embarrassment to us"? Would that help you to do your best?

A better way would be for your parents, the night before you leave home, to fix you your favorite meal, then sit down with you and tell you how proud they are of you, how proud they will always be of you, no matter what, and how much they will always love and believe in you.

Wouldn't that be far more likely to elicit your best shot in college? The second scenario is the way of love, and we believe that it is the basis of Christian ethics. In his Letter to the Romans, Paul speaks at length about the great love and forgiveness that is present in Christ. "There is therefore now no condemnation for those who are in Christ Jesus" (Romans 8:1). Then, in chapter 12, Paul inserts a decisive "therefore": "I appeal to you *therefore*...by the mercies of God, to present your bodies as a living sacrifice, holy and acceptable to God.... Do not be conformed to this world but be transformed by the renewing of your minds.... Let love be genuine;...extend hospitality to strangers.... Live in harmony....

115

Do not repay anyone evil for evil" (Romans 12:1–2a, 9a, 13b, 16a, 17a, emphasis added).

A Christian's ethic arises out of a Christian's faith. Because God has so loved us in Christ, we want to do all we can to return that love through the way we live.

One evening Will was leading a discussion among some students at Duke on the issue of academic integrity. Most of the students agreed that they would never think of cheating in the classroom. Some said that they were simply afraid they might get caught, and that fear was their main motivation for not cheating. Others recalled that the Ten Commandments say clearly, "You shall not steal"; and since cheating is a form of stealing, they therefore did not cheat.

One student said, "As a Christian, I am trying to follow Jesus, trying each day to, as the song says, 'Follow Him more nearly, see Him more clearly, love Him more dearly, day by day.' I don't want to do anything that would disappoint Jesus or the incredible faith He has placed in me by calling me to follow Him. I don't cheat because I don't want to betray His trust in me."

That strikes us as a Christian view of morality at its most basic. Think of our good deeds as our songs of praise to Christ, our hymns of gratitude.

❖ HELP IN DECIDING WHAT'S RIGHT ❖

The good news is that you don't have to go it alone when it comes to deciding how you ought to live as a Christian.

Though the answer to "What should I do?" might not be simple and clear in every case, and though we Christians may have some lively debates over just what Jesus would have us do in a given situation, God has given us much help in deciding how to live holy lives:

1. *The Bible* continues to be the main source of a Christian's ethical guidance. The Bible, despite any of its difficulties, continues to point us in the right direction. It may not tell you just how much of your income you ought to give to the work of God (in some places it says that 10 percent, a tithe, is a good place to start). But it does keep reminding you that everything you have is a gift from God, and that all of your possessions belong to God and therefore ought to be used with gratitude and responsibility.

The Bible may not tell you exactly how far to go in terms of physical intimacy when you are dating someone, but it will tell you that sex is a gift of God, a powerful force that can either enhance or ruin a life. The Bible makes it abundantly clear that sex should be confined to marriage and that is to be used for the glory of God and not just for our own selfish purposes.

2. *Your own reason* can help you to think through some situations as you weigh alternatives, gather the facts, and estimate the consequences. God gave you a mind. Use it. Ask a Christian friend or the members of your Bible study group to help you think through your tough decisions.

3. *Your church* can help. Make an appointment to talk things

over with your pastor. Pastors are there to help members of their congregations live faithful Christian lives. Probably the tough decision that you face has been faced by others before you. Your pastor can help you think about your decision in terms of the ethical teachings of your church, drawing upon the collective wisdom of the saints past and present.

Keep reminding yourself that you are a sinner, but a forgiven sinner. It is not your task to be perfect, to always make the right decision, and to always act in such a way that makes the world work. That is God's job, not yours. Your job is to do the best you can, to seek God's will for your life through prayer and study, then to go ahead and live. Act as courageously and boldly as you can, and leave the rest to God.

When Christians give to the poor or serve the less fortunate, stand up for justice or make peace, remain faithful or deny their lustful thoughts, we do so for much the same reason that Christians love to sing. We do it for love. We do it as our way of praising God, in all that we do, for the wonderful reality that God has called even us to be part of the Kingdom. Our code of ethics is akin to our worship. Our good deeds are part of our praise.

AM I SUPPOSED TO TRY TO CONVERT PEOPLE TO CHRISTIANITY?

◆ **The Good News Has Cosmic Dimensions**

God's Kingdom on Earth

Christians Are Called to Change Society

The Revolution *Will* Succeed

◆ **The Good News Defeats the Fear of Death**

I say live and let live! Why are some people so insecure that they have to make everyone around them agree with them about what they believe?

Intro

Great Commission Matt. 28

Jes[us] ... [th]e world and preac[h] ... of everyone (Matt ... and straight-forwa[rd] ... [se]ems to be a part c[of] ... [be]fore, carrying out th[e] ... [m]ore difficult than y[ou] ... [ca]mpus, there are outcries against evangelical student groups that try to win nonbelievers to the Christian faith. When Southern Baptists, at one of their recent conventions, targeted Jews for their evangelism outreach, many rabbis called the campaign "insensitive" and complained that this was just another attempt to wipe out the Jewish community.

Any of us who witness to our faith will have to do so

against a background of bad images generated by televange-lists who come across as money-grubbing hucksters and hellfire-and-brimstone preachers. But regardless of objections to the contrary, every Christian is expected to be a witness for Jesus and to tell others what He has done and will do for those who become committed to Him. Evangelism is a must for Christians, and if we are really infused with the Holy Spirit, as were the apostles in Bible times, we cannot help but share what we have personally experienced in our relationship with God.

When something very good happens to you, it is only natural for you to share that good news with everyone, particularly with people you love. So Mark begins his Gospel with "The beginning of the good news [gospel] of Jesus Christ" (Mark 1:1). Good news demands to be shared with anyone who will listen. Evangelism may be defined in a variety of ways, but one thing it always involves is *letting people know the good news about what God has done and is doing in the world.*

❖ THE GOOD NEWS HAS COSMIC DIMENSIONS ❖

Human history is not an absurdity. The good news is that history is going somewhere wonderful, and God is taking it there. Eventually, God will triumph over all the forces of evil that seem so omnipresent. In the end, says Scripture, everything will be made right:

> I pray that the God of our Lord Jesus Christ, the Father of glory, may give you a spirit of wisdom and revelation as you come to know him, so that, with the eyes of your heart enlightened, you may know what is the hope to which he has called you, what are the riches of his glorious inheritance among the saints, and what is the immeasurable greatness of his power for us who believe, according to the working of his great power. God put this power to work in Christ when he raised him from the dead and seated him at his right hand in the heavenly places, far above all rule and authority and power and dominion, and above every name that is named, not only in this age but also in the age to come. And he has put all things under his feet and has made him the head over all things for the church, which is his body, the fullness of him who fills all in all. (Ephesians 1:17–22)

Or, as one of our friends puts it, "The good news is that God is going to get back what belongs to God."

That means that all social institutions and cultural systems someday will be transformed into instruments that will embody God's love and justice. The Bible describes this as a done deal because the outcome is so sure, but the various governments, corporations, labor unions, media systems, etc., that constitute the principalities and powers are still in need of recognizing that Christ is their Lord and that they must come into obedience to His will. As God carries out this great design for the future of the world, we are invited to participate, and one of the ways we do this is through evangelism. In evangelism we not only declare this good news about the new world that's coming but we also invite people to join God in creating that new world. In evangelism we not only speak, but also enact the good news. We invite people to join in God's great revolution. God is going to get back what belongs to God, and a major way God does this is through *you*—through your words, your witness, and your life.

In evangelism, we invite people to join in God's great revolution.

You may think it strange that we should start the discussion about evangelism by declaring what God is doing in the world, but the decision to do so is deliberate. Americans, with their overemphasis on individualism, have been prone to make evangelism into something that is only personal. We want in no way to mislead you into thinking that the good news we are to declare to the world doesn't involve eternal life for the individual who believes and makes a life commitment to Christ. Nor do we want in any way to deny that there is a dark and awesome abyss for those who reject the free gift of salvation offered by Christ.

It is just that the gospel is more than a way to heaven for those individuals who say "yes" to the call of Christ. It has cosmic dimensions. It transcends the egoistic interests of people who are concerned only about saving their own necks by escaping the damnation of the lost. As Christians, we are required to make such things known, but there is more to evangelism than this. If you think evangelism is only about getting individuals "saved," then consider what the apostle Paul says: "The creation itself will be set free from its bondage to decay and will obtain the freedom of the glory of the children of God" (Romans 8:21).

When you evangelize, you also invite men and women to surrender their lives to Christ so that God can work through them to change the world. The salvation message you are called to declare is that God *so loved the world* (John 3:16)! The word world is *cosmos* in Greek, the language in which the Scripture was originally written. This is a declaration that God loves not only people, but the whole world and everything that's in it.

It means that God loves the natural world and calls upon us to work to prevent environmental destruction. It also means that God loves the institutions of society, ranging from the family to economic institutions, such as the AFL-CIO and Microsoft, and He invites us to be a Church that is at work in the world transforming these institutions into optimum instruments of blessing for all humanity. It means that God loves the school you attend and expects you to be at work as an agent of change so your school delivers all the good it is supposed to give both to students and to the larger society.

God's Kingdom on Earth

Those who are willing to let God change their lives will find themselves "led by the Spirit" into participating with God in moving society toward the glorious future envisioned when Jesus declared that the Kingdom of God was at hand: "The time is fulfilled, and the Kingdom of God has come near; repent, and believe the good news" (Mark 1:15).

You will find that when Jesus started His preaching ministry some two thousand years ago, He came declaring that the Kingdom of God was at hand (Matthew 10:7; Mark 1:15; Luke 4:43). In Matthew, because the audience of this book was Jewish, the phrase "the kingdom of heaven" is used. The Jews were reluctant to use the word *God,* so Matthew used "heaven" as a code word when referring to God. But the phrases "the kingdom of God" and "the kingdom of heaven" were the same thing. When Jesus taught His disciples to pray, He taught them to pray for God's Kingdom to come *on earth* as it is in heaven (Matthew 6:10). His Kingdom is no "pie-in-the-sky-when-you-die" sort of thing, like some neo-Marxists on your campus may mockingly claim. It is a kingdom that is to be realized in history. It is something God wants to see happen in the here and now.

The Kingdom begins as Jesus transforms individuals into Kingdom people—who call Jesus "Lord" and seek to do His will in the world. This emphasis on personal salvation is something liberal theologians in the Church sometimes neglect. But there is also a social dimension to it. The Kingdom of God also encompasses the institutions of society, which means that in addition to people needing to be transformed into what God wants them to be, social institutions also must be transformed into what God wants them to be. This latter emphasis is often missed by evangelical theologians. The two emphases belong together. The Kingdom of God is a transformed people living in a transformed social order.

Christians are Called to Change Society

One of the primary reasons Christ delivers us from sin is so He can have a people through which He can work out His plan to change the society into the society it ought to be. God wants us to go to work endeavoring to bring His will to bear upon the family, the workplace, educational institutions, the media, the political sphere, and the economic structures of society. Whenever the question comes up as to whether one can live out a Christian vocation in law, in the arts, in government, or in education, the answer has to be "Of course!" Jesus calls us to be a transforming leaven in each of these sectors of society. To do so is to be an evangelist, because through word and deed you are an instrument and an expression of what God is doing to make His Kingdom come on earth.

The Revolution *Will* Succeed

To be Christian is to participate in a revolution designed by God and also to give to the rest of the world the good news that this revolution will succeed. We have the promise from Scripture that in the end, the Church, that body of believers working to sign, to signal, to witness the transformation of the world into the kind of world God wants it to be, will win out over the forces of darkness: "The kingdom of the world has become the kingdom of our Lord and of his Messiah, and he will reign forever and ever" (Revelation 11:15). Evangelism is making this good news known. Anytime you speak or live out that good news, you are an evangelist.

During the sixties, while Tony was teaching at the University of Pennsylvania, he was caught up in the great social causes that inspired the students of that time. Young people in his classes were filled with hope and optimism and were convinced that a new social order marked by justice for all was about to break loose. Tony personally identified with their confidence that racism, sexism, militarism, and other forms of oppression could be overcome. He shared with them the vision of the future so powerfully articulated by Martin Luther King, Jr. in his famous "I Have a Dream" speech.

But things did not change as quickly as those students thought they would. The government and the economic system were not as easily amenable to transformation as those young people had imagined they would be. He watched as students became disillusioned, gave up their idealistic visions of the future, and turned to the narcissistic aspirations of yuppyism. They stopped believing that the world could be made good and settled for dreams of personal, professional, and materialistic success.

Now when Tony meets some of his former students from the sixties and early seventies, they are surprised that he continues to plug away for the old causes and that he is still enthusiastically committed to changing the world. Tony tells them of the good news that there is still hope and that things will change, and he tries to convince them that the kingdoms of this world *will* become the Kingdom of our God. But they usually just smile wistfully and dismiss him as naive. Evangelism is declaring to such skeptical and sometimes cynical former revolutionaries the good news that "it's not over 'till it's over." Evangelism is preaching that, when history is over, it will be the story of a God who triumphed and made the world into the peaceable kingdom described by the prophets (see Isaiah 65:17ff). Evangelism is being, in Desmond Tutu's words, "a prisoner of hope." In the midst of all this optimistic hope, we must not be deluded into thinking we can complete this transformation of society. That is what the second coming of Christ is all about. Christ is initiating a social revolution through His people, but it is a revolution that will be brought to completion (Philippians 1:6) only when He returns—and He *is* coming back in bodily form.

During World War II if you had asked members of the French Underground how they expected to overcome the powerful Nazi army that dominated their country, they would have said, "You should know that even as we speak a huge invasion force is being assembled on the other side of the English Channel. We do not know when it will happen, but someday soon they will sweep across the water, join us, and carry us to victory."

In a parallel manner, when I am asked how I expect the people of God to overcome the evil forces that seem in control of the principalities and powers and the rulers of this age, I say, "You should know that even as we speak a huge invasion force, consisting of Christ and His mighty army, is being assembled and someday (I know not when) a trumpet will sound, and His force will sweep into time and space and carry us to victory." That is part of the good news we declare to the world.

Ironically, it is when an individual stops worrying about his or her personal salvation and gets caught up in the work God wants to do in the world that a sense of personal salvation becomes a felt reality. Jesus made that very clear when He said: "Those who want to save their life will lose it, and those who lose their life for my sake, and for the sake of the gospel, will save it" (Mark 8:35).

The more preoccupied with self you become, the more the sense of spiritual fulfillment associated with personal salvation slips away. On the other hand, the more you surrender to Christ and join in God's crusades for justice and love in the world, the more you realize all the individual blessings God intends for you. When Jesus called people to follow Him, it was primarily to take up the cross (i.e., make the necessary sacrifices) and become His disciples. He promised spiritual rewards for those who would join Him in declaring and building the new social order.

> **Evangelism is an announcement, in word and deed, that the whole world has shifted on its axis.**

Evangelism is an announcement, in word and deed, that the whole world has shifted on its axis, that the whole direction of history has turned, that Jesus Christ reigns. Now. Evangelism is declaring that the Kingdom of God is already dawning among us. It is the declaration of a new social order that is breaking loose in the here and now. You will find, in your ministry of evangelism, that people will respond far more readily to an invitation to find meaning for their lives in trying to change the world and impacting the lives of others with loving service than they will to threats of damnation.

❖ THE GOOD NEWS DEFEATS ❖ THE FEAR OF DEATH

But even as we emphasize the cosmic dimensions of the salvation story that we declare in evangelism, we don't want to minimize the good news of a personal deliverance from the threat of death and the fear of hell. Most of you are much younger than we are, and the consciousness of encroaching death may not haunt you. There is a kind of denial of death that probably enables you to put it out of your mind.

Psychologists like Ernest Becker contend that young people usually have subconscious defenses against their own mortality but that, as we grow older, these defenses break down. Old guys like us have to make noise on New Year's Eve in order to drown out the macabre sounds of grass growing over our graves. To someone who is sixty-five, death is not simply an interesting topic that is discussed on Oprah's show. Instead, it is a reality that slowly permeates the consciousness. When Tony puts his head down on the pillow at night, he often says to himself, "Tony, you're one day closer!"

Such morbid thoughts could sap our energies and leave us devoid of joy. They probably would, except for the wonderful truth that Jesus has given us victory over the fear of death. As you surrender to the infusing presence of the Holy Spirit, it is possible to sense an inner assurance that you are a child of God, assured of eternal life. The Bible says: "It is that very

Spirit bearing witness with our spirit that we are children of God" (Romans 8:16).

This inner conviction that when life is over, something even better is waiting on the other side of silence, takes away much of the psychological threat of death that otherwise would oppress you. The apostle Paul made this point loud and clear when he wrote: " 'Where, O death, is your victory? Where, O death, is your sting?' The sting of death is sin, and the power of sin is the law. But thanks be to God, who gives us the victory through our Lord Jesus Christ" (1 Corinthians 15:55–57).

Governor Jesse Ventura of Minnesota has told the press that religion is for weaklings and cowards. But he has not yet come to the point in his life when death is real to him, or else he would know what Shakespeare's Hamlet knew: that in the face of death, "conscience doth make cowards of us all." When Governor Ventura realizes that death is imminent and that there is no psychological defense mechanism to ward off its reality, he may then realize that he, too, is weak and afraid. We have seen people who spoke eloquently and bravely about dying but were reduced to trembling and terror when their own time for dying came. Some who seem to be strong prove to be cowards when the ultimate enemy, death, is about to swallow them up. Death really is, in Paul's words, "the last enemy" (1 Corinthians 15:26). Jesus is the Great Physician who can heal the malady Soren Kierkegaard once labeled "the sickness unto death." Jesus tells us that if we do not think we have this sickness, then we do not need such a physician (Matthew 9:12–13). We believe Jesus said what He did with the full knowledge that the arrogant men to whom He spoke would one day face the dark hour of death and know the fear they had long denied. The salvation story Jesus calls you to declare is a message of hope that can dispel those fears.

Bill and Gloria Gaither wrote this beloved gospel hymn about the hope we have in Christ.

> Because He lives I can face tomorrow;
> Because He lives all fear is gone;
> Because I know He holds the future;
> And life is worth the living just because He lives.

That is the good part of the Easter good news you bring when you evangelize.

If you really believe the good news about what God can do for individual people and society, you will have to become an evangelist!

Evangelism is declaring the good news about what Jesus has already accomplished through His death and resurrection, what He can do in the lives of all who allow Him to transform them, and what He will do through His people to make the world into what it ought to be. If you declare that message, you *are* an evangelist!

HOW CAN I LISTEN TO A SERMON AND GET SOMETHING OUT OF IT?

7 HOW CAN I LISTEN TO A SERMON AND GET SOMETHING OUT OF IT?

I confess that I don't always get much out of a sermon on Sunday. There's this guy up there talking, and those in the audience have no opportunity for dialogue or feedback. It's just a lecture. What am I missing?

We'll admit that a sermon is an odd kind of communication. It is one-way, authoritarian communication in a single medium with no opportunity to talk back. Most of us are accustomed to the images of television, the multiple sounds of radio, and the interactive dimension of computers. As a college student, you know you tend to learn more through discussion in a seminar than by sitting and listening to a lecture. How, then, is it possible to listen to a sermon and get something out of it? Why is Christianity so tied to this act of worship?

We can't deny it. A Christian is a person who, among other things, needs to know how to listen to a sermon. There does seem to be something about the Christian faith that makes preaching central. When Jesus began His ministry, according to the Gospel of Luke, what did He do? He went to a synagogue (Luke 4:16–30), took up the scroll of the prophet Isaiah, and read from it. And then He preached. Jesus said, "The Spirit of the Lord is upon me…to bring good news to the poor…recovery of sight to the blind."

"From that time Jesus began to proclaim, 'Repent, for the kingdom of heaven has come near'"(Matthew 4:17). Jesus is portrayed as a preacher, someone who proclaims a message. In fact, the Christian word *gospel* means "good news."

Much of the Christian faith is involved in announcement, *kerygma*, proclamation of good news. The preacher is a herald. A herald does not make up his speech. A herald announces something that has happened. What has happened is that God has come into the world as Jesus the Christ. A good sermon always says something about that.

Paul says, "So faith comes from what is heard, and what is heard comes through the word of Christ" (Romans 10:17). The Christian faith is an auditory, acoustical phenomenon. The Christian faith does not come by taking long walks out in the woods or rummaging around in your ego or sitting quietly and thinking on spiritual things in the quietness of your dormitory room. The Christian faith comes through hearing, by someone telling you something you would not have known had not someone cared enough to tell you.

"In the beginning was the Word, and the Word was with God, and the Word was God" (John 1:1). The gospel is not self-derived. It is not some vague, religious feeling that arises from within. It is something that must be told. It is news that you would not know. Faith comes through speaking and hearing. The gospel is good news that stays news.

✧ THE ROLE OF THE PREACHER— ✧ PROCLAIMING THE WORD OF GOD

A preacher is someone who is called by God and the church to speak this good news. How does this happen? First, a preacher goes to the Bible and listens to Scripture on behalf of the congregation, hoping to make a discovery, to hear something that can be heard only by listening to Scripture. Then the preacher stands in the pulpit on Sunday and announces that discovery to the congregation. Preachers must therefore study the Scriptures, living *with* them and *in* them, listening carefully to the biblical text. So preachers often learn Greek and Hebrew in order to be better equipped to listen to the Bible in its original languages. While each Christian is responsible for going to God's Word for him- or herself, the preacher has a special obligation to look deeply into the Word of God and apply it to the needs of the congregation.

Moving Us from One Place to Another

We admit that though it is a challenge to make Jesus into someone who is boring, sometimes preachers succeed. Sometimes sermons go on too long. Our minds wander. We find it hard to be attentive. Modern people are accustomed to listening to TV sound bites of a couple of seconds, not to thirty-minute sermons. Many of our attention spans are no longer than the span between two television commercials. Therefore listening to sermons can be quite a challenge.

More honestly speaking, it is difficult to listen to sermons not because we lack the skills to sit still for a public address but because sermons make a claim upon us. In the sermon, the preacher is a herald, announcing something that has happened in the world. What has happened in the world is Jesus Christ. Now that God has come into the world as Jesus the Christ, the whole world has changed. A preacher stands up and proclaims a different sovereign than the one we are accustomed to obeying. The preacher wants us to exchange our citizenship; he wants to move us from one country to another, to a place called the Kingdom of God.

Making the Bible Relevant

Preachers must also listen carefully for the congregational context, being attentive to the needs and questions of their people. Preachers read novels, go to movies, and talk with others in order to learn and be able to speak the language of their congregation. It has been said that the preacher stands with the Bible in one hand and today's newspaper in the other. And as we have said in the previous chapter, the Bible can be a great challenge. Many of us are not that familiar with great portions of Scripture. It is the preacher's job to make Scripture come alive for us, to speak to us. In the sermon, the Bible becomes

God's Word addressed to us in our time and place. That can be a great challenge for the preacher.

Submitting to the Word of God

In preaching, the preacher must submit to the biblical text. The preacher doesn't always preach that which he or she personally understands or believes. Rather it is the duty of the preacher to preach what the Bible preaches, to preach the faith of the Church.

A preacher friend of ours was shaking the hands of people at the door of his church as they were departing at the end of the Sunday service. One of the members said, "I really didn't care for what you said in your sermon today."

The preacher replied, "Do you really think *I* liked what I said? This is what the Gospel of Matthew has to say to us, not what I have to say. I stand under the same judgment of this text as you." A preacher is a servant of the Word of God. The reason that teaching is difficult to assimilate, hear, and receive is not simply because it is an ancient word from a world of sheep and shepherds, demons and devils, but also because it is a word that challenges the world where we live.

Have some sympathy with us preachers, won't you? It's not an easy way to make a living. Put yourself in our shoes. There Will stands on a Sunday, preaching in a chapel in the middle of a large university. Knowing that the congregation will include a large number of students and young adults, he rummages about in the Gospels attempting to find some biblical text that

141

might speak to his audience. He's got it! Matthew 19:16–26. Here, Jesus meets a man who not only is very religious but who has kept *all* the commandments of God since he was a kid. Also, he is "young." (Sure, Mark says that he was a "man." Luke calls him a "ruler." But Will knows he's speaking to a group of nineteen year olds, so he goes with Matthew. The guy in the story was a rich, *young* man.) He wants to have "eternal life," the things that Jesus is offering. What does he need to do to get it? He is big on doing, this young man. He hasn't only kept all of the commandments, he's also done well economically. Matthew implies that he is rich.

"Jesus said to him, 'If you wish to be perfect, go, sell your possessions, and give the money to the poor, and you will have treasure in heaven; then come, follow me' " (Matthew 19:21).

With that, the young man gets really depressed and leaves, prompting Jesus to say that it is as easy for a rich person to enter His Kingdom as for a fully loaded dump truck to get in a mailbox—or some words to that effect.

Do you think it's easy to preach that to a group of smart, upwardly mobile, acquisitive young adults? It's the sort of Bible text that sends a preacher scurrying for something like "consider the lilies" or some other saying that is unlikely to get people mad at either Jesus or the preacher. Preaching, as great as it is, is not the end of the Christian life. It's the beginning. We are to be doers of the Word, not just good listeners (James 1:22). Sermons are not just meant to be heard; they are meant to be lived.

✦ THE PURPOSE OF THE SERMON— ✦ TRANSFORMATION

What is the difference between a sermon and a lecture? Is it that preachers sometimes shout while professors sound dull? No. One major difference is that while most lectures attempt to convey information, most sermons aim, in one way or another, at *transformation*; their purpose is to change who people are—how they think and what they do. The question behind the sermon is not "Do you agree?" but rather the more involving "Will you join up?" So a good question to ask yourself as you are listening to a sermon is "How is this sermon making a claim on my life?"

We are old enough to remember when the ending of nearly every worship service, in the churches where we grew up, was the "altar call." After the preacher had finished preaching, a hymn was sung and people were invited to come down to the altar rail and commit their lives to Christ. While few churches today end every service with an altar call, the ending of every sermon is a call to Christian commitment. A sermon is an implicit or explicit call to conversion, to change, to transformation.

Don't listen to sermons if you don't want to risk transformation!

Will was asked to have coffee and conversation with a student who wanted him to meet a sophomore, football-player friend of his. His friend had grown up in the church but, for some reason, had grown away from the church while in college. The conversation went something like this:

Will: So, have you come to Duke Chapel while you've been here? Have you heard me preach?

Sophomore: Nope.

Will: Aren't you at all curious about what we do on Sunday morning? We're Christians, so we talk a lot about the cross and failure, about blood and defeat. I would have thought those topics would be relevant to a Duke football player!

Sophomore: Oh, I know what you talk about in sermons. I went to church some when I was a kid.

Don't come in here If you don't want to risk being changed.

Will: Really? And what do you know about church from that?

Sophomore: As I recall, Christians are always trying to get people to change, to live better lives, to be better people. And, frankly, right now I'm fairly pleased with my life. I like myself right now. I'm having a good time here, and I don't want to change. Before I graduate, I might want to change, and if I do, I'll come to church. OK?

Will: I love that! That's got to be the best reason I ever heard for not coming to church! I'm going to do that in needlepoint, frame it, and put it over the door of the chapel: Don't Come in Here If You Don't Want to Risk Being Changed.

Conversion, transformation, being born again, is the name

of our game. No wonder some people avoid church. Others come expecting to have what they already believe confirmed.

Presenting an Alternative Cosmos

Church at its best is a Sunday assault upon our perceived, conventional world. Through the sermon, listeners are presented with an alternative world, with a cosmos that is counter to the one offered on MTV or the Home Shopping Channel. On Sunday morning, as we listen to a sermon, we are to lay our personal stories—as people in North America in the twenty-first century—alongside the authoritative biblical story. We should be attempting to read our lives in light of the gospel. The preacher usually spends some time "picking apart" or redescribing a Bible passage, then endeavors to help us apply that passage to our lives today.

It is interesting that we speak of a "Bible passage." A passage to where? Through the sermon, Bible passages come alive; they become a door that opens to us, a passage where we move from one state of life to another.

When you emerge from a really good movie, you sometimes have that strange experience of being genuinely surprised that it is still daylight and that you are still living in the same place you were living when you went into the theater. Your eyes squint at the light, and familiar things seem strange. The film has had its way with you, has transported you into another world in the space of a couple of hours. In a sense, because of the movie, you don't live in the same place where you once lived. You are in a different world. You are different. If you don't want to risk such movement, such transformation and conversion, then it is best to simply sleep through the sermon!

Sometimes people complain that a sermon is irrelevant to their lives—and it's true that some preachers fail to relate the biblical story to our own. Yet the sermon is not intended to be an artful reiteration of everything we already know and believe. The sermon's goal is to tell us something we might not yet believe. Yet many modern people have the nasty tendency of dismissing any information that offers a fundamental challenge to their world. "I've never seen anyone walk on water in Des Moines," they say. "Therefore, Jesus and Peter could not have walked on the Sea of Galilee."

So when someone says, "The trouble with that sermon was that it didn't talk about the life *I* live," well, that may be just the point. A good sermon doesn't just want to address you where you now live; it wants to move you to another place!

Training Us in a New Language

Sometimes students complain that preachers use big, strange, archaic words that are never heard outside of church—*redemption, atonement, justification,* and such. Why don't preachers talk in plain English?

In support of these complaints, we admit that Jesus rarely used big words like these in His sermons. Fortunately, Jesus told lots of stories and loved to use everyday experiences like banquets, salt, bread, and wine to illustrate. Preachers could learn from Jesus.

But in fairness to preachers, we need to note that a sermon is also training in a new language—the vocabulary and grammar of the Christian faith. You don't stroll into an introductory physics class and expect the professor to use only words and concepts that you already know. You expect to be confused by the new material. And though you may find it a real pain, you expect to memorize lists of new words and learn about new concepts so that one day, before the end of the semester, you will *be* a physicist.

Becoming a Christian is something akin to learning physics. It doesn't come naturally. You can't get this faith by drinking the water or breathing the air. You must sit for it; you must have it explained to you. Someone has got to tell it to you, and it may take some time before you can say, "I get it."

In fact, when it comes to our relationship to God in Christ, it's *never* quite right to say, "I got it." No, it's *God* who gets *you*. One way God gets us is by our learning and inculcating a new account of our lives. We learn new words to describe what's going on in the world and in us.

❖ HOW TO GET MORE OUT OF A SERMON ❖

We have some suggestions for you, for how you might get more out of the sermon.

Submit to the Words of the Sermon

We must be willing to risk laying our lives alongside the gospel. That can sometimes be painful. When, through a sermon, our little lives are held up to the honest light of the gospel, we are sometimes disturbed by what we see.

We are modern people who resist submission to anything. Our culture tells us that we are self-made men and women. We like to think that our lives are self-derived, that we are the sum of our choices, decisions, and actions. But Christian preaching is a sign that our lives are being shaped and formed by God. It's true that we must make decisions for God, but Scripture is mostly a story about God's decisions for us, about the way God keeps moving in human history, inexorably moving our lives toward His light. If you are unwilling to submit to that story, then preaching will be uninteresting for you. In church, we play a distinctive "language game." We get together on Sunday morning and open up the Scriptures, just as Luke 4 tells us Jesus did in Nazareth.

Expect Surprises

Expect a claim to be made on your life. Expect to be asked to change. After you hear a sermon, you might find yourself saying, "I never heard anything like this before." Of course you haven't heard this. This is new. This is God's way rather than the American way. (Where in North America would you expect to hear the gospel? MTV? Not likely.) Sermons expect, provoke, invoke change. If after hearing a sermon, you think, *If I really did what that preacher is suggesting, I could get hurt,* you are exactly right. Jesus said, up front, that whoever followed Him would also have to carry His cross.

Expect God to Speak to You

Remember, "faith comes by hearing." It is our rather astounding claim that through an ordinary person, speaking ordinary words, God gets to us, cuts through our defenses, and transforms our lives. The Holy Spirit gets into the preacher's sermons, making that sermon *your* sermon, and through it, you hear the very voice of God speaking to you. That's usually what people mean when they say to a preacher at the church door, "You really preached to me today!" They mean that the Holy Spirit used the sermon as God's word to them. And when that happens, it's wonderful.

Faith really does come by hearing—by God's grace, and by the work of the Holy Spirit. When that happens, you will be able to say, "Man, you really preached to me today."

And the Word of God will dwell in you richly.

8 WHAT'S THE POINT OF WORSHIP?

Frankly, I just don't get much out of the Sunday-morning thing. I like some of the music, particularly when it's contemporary. But most of it doesn't do anything for me. Am I supposed to feel something? And isn't Christianity more about doing than about sitting and listening? What is the good of all the praying and the singing and the sitting and listening?

"What is the chief end of humanity?"

That's the question asked in the catechism of some churches. The proper answer: *The chief end of humanity is to glorify God and enjoy God forever.*

That's why we have been put on this earth. That's the point of your life—to glorify and enjoy God. With this as our "chief end," it's not difficult to understand why some see the Christian faith as strange. Marva Dawn, a Christian theologian, calls Christian worship "a royal waste of time," claiming that worship is the pointless activity of being with, hanging out with, royalty.

Throughout our exploration of the Christian faith in this book, we have spoken of God's love in Christ and our response to that love. We have said that we respond to God's love with our loving acts of service toward those in need in the Church and in the world. But we are called not simply to *obey* God; we are also called to *glorify* Him. And above all, we are called to *enjoy* Him. We are called to *worship*.

✤ WE DO IT FOR LOVE ✤

If you have ever been in love, you know that love is not love if it is simply a matter of obeying rules, running errands, and performing duties. Some things we do just because we enjoy being in the presence of the beloved. We sing songs, write poetry, dance, clap our hands, share food, or simply prop up our feet and do nothing but enjoy hanging out with each other. It is in these purposeless, pointless moments of sheer enjoyment that we come very close to the purpose and point of love.

If someone asks us as Christians, "What's the purpose of your worship? Why do you Christians gather on Sunday and sing songs, dress up, kneel, march in processions, clap your hands, shed tears, speak, eat, shout, and listen to sermons?" we could only say, "Because we are in love."

But we Americans tend to be pragmatic, practical people. We are utilitarians, always asking of every experience, "What good will this do me? What can I get out of this?"

Let's say you're walking hand in hand with your beloved on a spring night across campus. At some point, in the moonlight, the two of you gaze into one another's eyes and kiss. Now imagine that some bystander who had never been in love sees you and asks, "What good will that do you? What are you going to get out of that?"

Obviously, the dummy has never ever been in love.

The most serious, most delightful business of Christians—when you get right down to it—is that loving work of glorifying God and enjoying Him forever. In other words—*worship*. Whether we are glorifying and enjoying God in church through our music, sermons, baptisms, and prayers or outside of church in our social concern, witnessing, and charity, it is all for one purpose: to glorify God and enjoy Him forever.

The very last Psalm, the last song in the hymn book of Israel, is this wonderfully pointless shout of praise:

> Praise the Lord! Praise God in his sanctuary; praise him in his mighty firmament! Praise him for his mighty deeds; praise him according to his surpassing greatness! Praise him with trumpet sound; praise him with lute and harp! Praise him with tambourine and dance; praise him with strings and pipe! Praise him with clanging cymbals; Praise him with loud clashing cymbals! Let everything that breathes praise the Lord! Praise the Lord! (Psalm 150)

❖ THE VALUE OF SACRAMENTS ❖ AND ORDINANCES

God's love is demonstrated most powerfully through *sacraments* and *ordinances*.

Sacraments and ordinances are signs and symbols of the presence and action of God. Christians observe two sacraments or ordinances, two "acts of love" that Jesus gave His disciples:

baptism and the *Lord's Supper* (or Holy Communion). In these symbolic gestures we taste, touch, feel, know, and experience the grace of God. Through them, we know the love of God to be a present reality in our lives.

The Lord's Supper

The sacraments speak of mysteries too deep for words or mere understanding. As one person said of the Lord's Supper, "I would rather experience it than understand it." In another sense, the meaning of this sacrament is close to the most common, everyday experiences in life.

It was at the end of His earthly ministry that Jesus gave us this powerful symbol of love—a meal with loving friends. "For I received from the Lord what I also handed on to you, that the Lord Jesus on the night when he was betrayed took a loaf of bread, and when he had given thanks, he broke it and said, 'This is my body that is for you. Do this in remembrance of me.' In the same way he took the cup also, after supper, saying, 'This cup is the new covenant in my blood. Do this, as often as you drink it, in remembrance of me.'" (1 Corinthians 11:23–25). The Lord's Supper means everything that any meal means: love, fellowship, hospitality, and joy. The *bread* in this meal symbolizes hunger and nourishment, human need and divine gifts. The *wine* is a rich and red symbol of spirit, vitality, life, and blood. Paul told the divided church at Corinth, "Because there is one bread, we who are many are one body, for we all partake of the one bread" (1 Corinthians 10:17). These mealtime meanings are given added significance because, at this meal, we commune with the risen Christ who joins us at our table.

Baptism

Jesus also gave His followers a sacrament of His love to share with the rest of the world—baptism, the sign of initiation into the Christian faith. "Go therefore and make disciples of all nations, baptizing them in the name of the Father and of the Son and of the Holy Spirit" (Matthew 28:19). Baptism means everything that water means: cleansing, birth, power, refreshment, life—even death. These natural benefits of water are given added significance because the baptismal water is given "in the name of Jesus." Paul spoke of baptism as if we were drowning our old lives so that we might be born to new life. "Do you not know that all of us who have been baptized into Christ Jesus were baptized into his death? Therefore we have been buried with him by baptism into death, so that, just as Christ was raised from the dead by the glory of the Father, so we too might walk in newness of life" (Romans 6:3–4).

The sacraments speak of mysteries too deep for words or mere understanding.

❖ ACTIONS AND SYMBOLS ❖
EXPRESS ACTS OF LOVE

"Don't tell me, show me," pleads a song in *My Fair Lady*. To say "I love you" is to say something wonderful, but sometimes we want more than words. We communicate not only through speech but also through action. "Actions speak louder than words," we sometimes say. In our discussion of the value of sermons, we pointed out that Christians are big on speaking and listening—but we are also big on action, demonstration, and performance.

Sometimes you may hear folks say of a church at worship, "They are just putting on a show. They are just having a performance."

Such words are meant as criticism. Yet in a way, that's exactly what we want our worship to be. We want to do more than sit and listen. We want to get into the act with Jesus. We want to join in His work in the world; we want to perform and enact our faith.

In the Bible, God not only says, "I love you," through the words of the Law, the prophets, the sermons of Jesus, and the letters of Paul; God's love is also demonstrated, enacted, performed.

Actions convey deep meaning. A flag, a handshake, a kiss, a wedding ring—these are the symbols of love that say more than mere words can express. A cross, kneeling for prayer, applause, a shout of joy—these are ways of letting actions and symbols speak louder than words in our worship of God.

Sacraments are everyday objects like bread and water and everyday actions like eating and bathing that, when incorporated in worship, convey our love for our God. They are the means by which we express feelings too deep for words.

Not only do we use these objects and actions in worship to show our love for God; God also uses such symbols to show His love for us. Our Creator knows that we creatures depend on demonstrations of divine love. So God uses everyday things we can understand to show us love that defies understanding.

God uses every-day things we can understand to show us love that defies understanding.

God gives us Christ as the supreme visible and tangible symbol, expressing and revealing His love for us. "And the Word became flesh and lived among us, and we have seen his glory as of a father's only son, full of grace and truth.... From his fullness we have all received, grace upon grace.... No one has ever seen God. It is God the only Son, who is close to the Father's heart, who has made him known" (John 1:14–18).

You can think of other acts of worship besides the sacraments that are also acts of love: confirmation, a wedding, a funeral, sermons, prayers, hymns, altar calls. In all these activities, we reach out to God in love only to find that, in love, God has been reaching out to us.

✧ THE ROLE OF RITUAL IN MEETING WITH GOD ✧

Two people meet one another on the sidewalk. Their eyes meet. Will they greet one another, encounter one another, or pass by silently?

One person extends her hand, the other responds. They shake hands, embrace.

"How are you getting along?" he asks.

"Fine," she responds. "And you?"

The handshake, the embrace, the traditional words of meeting are a ritual that enables us to meet one another. Without the ritual, without the familiar, predictable pattern, we might not risk the meeting. We would not know how to come into the presence of another. The ritual helps us overcome the distance between us. It ends the separation.

Sunday-Morning Drama

The church also has a pattern of familiar words and actions whereby we are enabled to meet both other people and God. You might think of our Sunday morning worship pattern as a drama, a drama of meeting. On Sunday we follow a script—a pattern of words and actions that begins, moves from one act to another, and then comes to a conclusion.

Who are the actors in this drama of worship? The minister, the choir, the organist or pianist, and the ushers? This makes the congregation the audience. Is that the way it ought to be? No. The members of the *congregation* are actors in this divine-human drama. We are not to come on Sunday morning as though we were going to a movie or play, as though we were coming to passively watch the stars act their parts. We are there to join together in prayer and song. We are the actors rather than the audience.

Our worship leaders, like the minister, choir, organist, and ushers, are to help us worship, not to worship for us. They are there to invite us to sing, to cue us when it is time to kneel or pray or speak, to lead us so that we can all join together with one heart and voice in praise to God. When we experience Sunday worship as a time to walk in, flop down in our seat, and passively watch someone else meet God, we have not experienced the fullness of Christian worship.

The Pattern of Worship

Sometimes critics say of a church, "It is just too ritualistic." But ritual is a basic, unavoidable part of human behavior. Why do we have a set pattern for our worship services? Why do we often print an order of worship in our bulletin that we follow on Sunday morning? Why does your church usually worship in much the same way every Sunday? Because it is easier to gather for worship if we have some predictable pattern, some familiar pattern that brings us together.

If you sing a solo, you can "do your own thing." You can sing in your own style and tempo. But if you are in a choir, if you want to make music with more than one voice, you must get together. Everyone follows the same set of notes, sings the same words. Private, solitary meetings with God have their place. We have stressed the value of personal study and devotions. But congregational worship on Sunday morning is a group time. It is a time for meeting, gathering with the Body of Christ, joining together with one voice, and coming before God.

To that end, we sing hymns together because it is fun to join our voices in shouts of praise. We pray together because our deepest needs and highest joys are generally those we share with others, and so we now join with others in sharing those needs and joys with God. We listen to God's Word together because the gospel is not addressed to us simply as solitary individuals but as the Body of Christ. We respond to the Word by saying a creed because our beliefs are not only the private thoughts of our hearts but are nurtured, corrected, expanded, challenged, and supported in fellowship with other Christians in the church. We sing ancient hymns because they are a gift from the saints who have lived the faith before us. This is why we generally find it helpful to have a pattern for our Sunday worship—so we can get it all together.

❖ GETTING IT TOGETHER IN WORSHIP ❖

When you hear your voice raised with others in the congregation, singing the hymn, you feel that a veil between heaven and earth, humanity and God, has been thrown back. You see what you were unable to glimpse in your work-a-day, Monday-through-Saturday world. It is as though heaven comes very close to you and a new, wondrous world opens up to you. You are able to say—as did your ancestor Jacob when heaven's ladder was lowered to within his reach—"Surely the LORD is in this place—and I did not know it!" (Genesis 28:16).

So much of the time in church is spent using words like *should* and *ought* and *must*. Sunday becomes the day when a burden of greater responsibility is heaped on your shoulders, the day when we gather and the preacher tell us what we ought to do.

The worship service includes the "service" we offer to God, but worship is also the service God renders to us. While we are busy praising God, God is responding to us. Faith is a gift, not our achievement. As we praise God, we are being formed into God's people. We are practicing the presence of God in such a way that, as God becomes more apparent to us on Sunday, God is surely more real to us on Monday.

Why do we do it? We do it because we are in love. The modern world teaches us to ask of every event and relationship, "Now what good will this do me?" The modern world teaches us to make ourselves the center of the world, that we have no more important project than ourselves.

Christian worship is countercultural to all this. We do it, not primarily to get something out of it, but to give something to it. We do it because we are in love.

Catholic novelist Walker Percy asked in his novel *Lost in the Cosmos,* "How can you survive in the cosmos, about which you know more and more while knowing less and less about yourself, this despite 10,000 self-help books, 100 psycho-therapists, and 100,000 Fundamentalist Christians?" The title of Percy's novel says it all: *Lost in the Cosmos: The Last Self-Help Book.* We seem to be more adept at scientifically penetrating the universe than we are at figuring out ourselves. We send a spacecraft far into the heavens, moving farther away from our world, and it seems as if we have given up trying to understand our world and have gone to look for other worlds. Science tells us a great many facts about the world yet restricts our ability to be amazed and to wonder. We know more and more about less and less. We have figured out everything about the world except that it is beautiful. We are lost, lost in the cosmos, wandering like exiles, aliens in our own land, drifting loose, unsteady.

Percy says that his novel is "the last self-help book." We live in a world of self-made men and women. Mother, I had rather do it myself. Most of us long to live do-it-yourself lives. And yet, despite our anxious, earnest efforts, our techniques for self-improvement, and our programs for self-betterment, we get the nagging feeling that what we most need, we are not able to do for ourselves. Wherein is our help?

In worship, we reach out to the God who, in Jesus, first reached out to us. We acknowledge that we do not have it within ourselves to save ourselves. Thus, in a self-help, lost world,

Sunday worship may be among the most countercultural, subversive acts of Christians.

Luke gives us one of the earliest glimpses of Christian worship: "All who believed were together and had all things in common; they would sell their possessions and goods and distribute the proceeds to all, as any had need. Day by day, as they spent much time together in the temple, they broke bread at home and ate their food with glad and generous hearts, praising God and having the goodwill of all the people. And day by day the Lord added to their number those who were being saved" (Acts 2:44–47). Note that this passage links what Christians do when they are

> **Sunday worship may be among the most countercultural, subversive acts of Christians.**

in church, praising God, with what Christians do the rest of the week in their lives in the world. It's all service. Our worship is an aspect of our ethics; our Christian ethics are another way of worshiping. We want to pray and sing in church on Sunday in such a way that our lives in the world Monday through Saturday become, in all we do and say, prayers and songs to God. We want to worship God on Sunday in such a way that our whole lives become worship. "Make a joyful noise to the Lord, all the earth. Worship the Lord with gladness; come into his presence with singing.... Enter his gates with thanksgiving, and his courts with praise. Give thanks to him, bless his name" (Psalm 100:1–2, 4).

AND WHAT ABOUT SEX?

9 AND WHAT ABOUT SEX?

It's like the worst thing you can do, right? Christians are really hung up on sex. How can they feel so bad about something that is so natural?

Despite what Dr. Ruth, Madonna, and the Playboy channel may have told you, sex, which God invented and designed to be good, often ends up bad. Author Frederick Buechner has said, "Sex is like nitroglycerin; it can either be used to heal hearts or to blow up bridges." Surprisingly, the Bible has something to say about how good sex goes bad.

Some time ago, a friend called Will to ask for help with her seventeen-year-old son.

"It's just terrible," she said. "He hasn't been to school for two weeks now. He just lies on the sofa, staring at the ceiling. He has lost nearly twenty pounds because he refuses to eat. He has even threatened suicide. I don't know what to do."

Will couldn't believe that the woman's son, whom he had known as a robust, energetic young man, could be in such a state. "What on earth is the problem?" he asked.

"He says he's depressed because his girlfriend has broken up with him."

"That's ridiculous," Will replied. "He can't be acting like that simply because his girlfriend broke up with him."

Will consented to spend an evening talking with the young man. When they met, Will could see what his mother had been talking about. He was emaciated, pale, and lethargic. Something catastrophic, something terrible, had caused this change to come over him. He and Will talked all evening, and gradually, he began to reveal his feelings. Midway through the conversation, Will said to himself, *As unbelievable as it seems, I think this boy is acting this way because his girlfriend broke up with him.*

The pain of rejected love, the heartache of romance denied, can be devastating. Thousands of young people end their lives in the misery and confusion brought on by unhappy encounters with the opposite sex. Some of you have exchanged promises to spend your life with someone only to have your dreams crumble in a wave of disillusionment, heartache, recrimination, and separation.

Increasing numbers of you have experienced divorce from the other side, as a child of divorcing parents. Will has talked with many young couples who say, "We've been thinking about marriage, but we just don't know. Our parents are divorced. Some of our high school friends who got married are already separated. Is it possible for men and women to live together in marriage anymore?"

In addition to the pain of broken promises and the seeming absence of lasting relationships, history has documented that relationships between men and women are often woefully unjust, that even the sacred institution of marriage has often legitimized the subjugation of women and the arrogance of men. Even today, some Christians attempt to justify women's submission by appeals to Scripture.

When asked about the sorry state of affairs between women and men, Jesus went on record as saying, "From the beginning it was not so" (Matthew 19:8). That is, let no one declare that relationships between men and women today in our culture are God's intended pattern for all time. Something has gone wrong, terribly wrong, between the sexes, says Jesus. God, in creating male and female, has (as God so often does) brought something together. "What God has joined together, let no one separate," Jesus warns (Matthew 19:6).

Let no one declare that relationships between men and women today are God's intended pattern for all time.

And yet, the fact that someone asked Jesus about separation between male and female two thousand years ago indicates that human separating of divine joining is an ancient problem. How did things get this way?

❖ HOW IT ALL BEGAN ❖

For the answer, we'll have to go back, back a long way, back beyond even Jesus, to the first, dim days of human history, to a story older than time:

> Then the Lord God said, "It is not good that the man should be alone; I will make him a helper as his partner." So out of the ground the Lord God formed every animal of the field and every bird of the air, and brought them to the man to see what he would call them; and whatever the man called every living creature, that was its name:…all cattle,…birds of the air, and…every beast of the field; but for the man there was not found a helper as his partner. (Genesis 2:18–20)

The Creator has made a creature, an earthling (the "man" here is not yet a "male," for male and female had not yet been created). This creature is to have "dominion" over all the plants and animals of creation. It talks; it thinks; it responds—obviously, it is a marvelous creature. But something is missing.

Without consulting the earthling, God declares, "It is not good that the man should be alone." (Possibly, Adam was quite happy to be left alone, but this is not God's way of doing things.) "I will make a companion (Genesis 2:18 TLB)," says

God. So God takes the dust and makes all sorts of interesting creatures—beasts, birds, every living thing. But alas, there was not found a companion fit for him. What God wants for this creature is not simply an assistant, a servant, a "helper" (as most translations unfortunately translate the Hebrew), but a companion, neither an inferior nor a superior but one who alleviates the pain of isolation, the loneliness of dominion.

This creature called "man" has been given power over creation—over all plants and animals. It can build and plan, execute, dominate, research, write dissertations, make war, run for office, and build. But alas, even in its power, the creature is plagued by loneliness. All of the animals are paraded before the creature. Yet the rich menagerie disappoints rather than delights. In spite of what the pet food commercials tell you, no fit companion is found even among the animals.

There must be some newness, some fresh creative act—not simply a refashioning of the dust as God did in the case of the man and the animals—but some stunning and unpredicted creativity. It is at this point, says Genesis, that God brought to life His bright idea of sex. From one earthling, God created male and female, diversifying and articulating the earthling in an exciting new way.

Thus, God at last brings to the earthling a suitable partner. Other creatures come from the dust. This one is built in an entirely new way, not derived from someone else, but, in the Hebrew, "built" up from a rib. Woman is the crowning event of creation, the mature handiwork of a great artisan, the complex fulfillment of humanity.

Oh, man is fine, as far as he goes. But in the woman, it all comes to completion. In her, humanity is complete.

The man greets this masterpiece of creation by exclaiming, "At last!" In a play on the Hebrew words, he says, "This is woman. I am man." (It is an exuberant, playful story.) "At last! You did a good job on the zebras, the giraffes, but now, wow!"

There are two distinct earthlings, man and woman. In saying, "This at last is bone of my bones and flesh of my flesh" (Genesis 2:23), the man is not claiming superiority for himself; that would be absurd, considering the lengths to which God has gone to create the woman. Rather, "this is...flesh of my flesh" speaks of the unity, solidarity, and mutuality he feels with this new creature. She is the missing half of his humanity. These creatures, male and female, are so bound to one another, flesh of flesh and bone of bones, that the writer is able to say, "Therefore a man leaves his father and his mother and clings to his wife, and they become one flesh" (Genesis 2:24).

❖ SEXUALITY AS IT WAS INTENDED ❖

Sexuality is thus for Genesis not a mark of division, as it is so often in these latter days, but a mark of oneness, wholeness, and unity. The woman is a gift—God's gift of life—so that the male and female, through sex, participate in the same act of creativity that formerly belonged only to God. They shall produce, in their union, other males and females. As a gift, woman is not controlled by man. He must move toward her to achieve union. In their joy of sex, they shall, in the biblical words, "cling to" one another and become "one flesh." In sex, God enables men and women to participate in some of the same divine creativity that God enjoys.

Mutuality, Not Subordination

Be careful. No text in Genesis (or likely in the entire Bible) has been more used, interpreted, and misunderstood than this text. It has been used in the defense of male domination of women: Women are derived from men, so the argument goes; therefore, women are inferior and subordinate to men. This, we hope you see, is a gross misreading of the plain facts of the story. The story isn't one of subordination and inferiority but rather one of *mutuality*. The union

Male and female, through sex, partici- pate in the same act of creativity that formerly belonged only to God.

of male and female—in sex, in marriage, in work, in play, in creativity, and in dominion of God's creation—is to be in response to the way God created them. In playful, childlike communion, the man and woman dwell in God's good garden. They are naked, says the writer, but not ashamed (Genesis 2:25). Here, in their mutuality, they are like innocent, playful children. As Jesus noted, this is how it was in the beginning. This is what God wanted.

God's Gift Perverted

Unfortunately, as is so often the case, this is not what God gets. The story moves on to the day when male and female disobey God and take matters into their own hands. Not content to be God's beloved creatures, they attempt to be gods unto themselves. The once idyllic life in the Garden abruptly ends. They are ashamed of their nakedness. The once bountiful garden becomes choked with weeds and thorns. The once mutualist man and woman become locked in the struggle of a superior and subordinate. Sex and childbearing—joyful, delightful gifts of God—become acts of anguish and pain. You know the story.

You know the story because we live it. The tragic results of our culture's subjugation of women are all around us in the battered wives, unfulfilled lives, and anger of so many. The bitter harvest of male domination is felt in the loneliness, the uncertainty, and the attenuated humanity of many men. Sex, which should be a joy and a delight, becomes a daily battle waged with the weapons of manipulation, seduction, coercion, violence, and perversity. Like so many of God's good gifts—money, knowledge, power—we pervert the gift of sex into our own selfish, lonely struggle for godlike power. Liberation becomes a fancy way of saying "loneliness," and in the words of a popular song, "Freedom's just another word for nothing left to lose." Free, liberated, on your own, looking out for number one, doing your own thing, scoring, making, laying, and getting—from the beginning, it was not so.

Sex Makes Us Whole

Some time ago, someone did a study of hundreds of men and women in marriage. The researchers found, somewhat to their surprise, that men were generally happier in marriage than women. When asked why they were happy in marriage, the men's comments went something like this: "My wife has helped unlock a part of me that I didn't know existed. She has helped me express my real feelings; she's helped me not be ashamed of how I feel. I would be only half a person without her."

We would like to think that the same could be said by women: "Without him, I'd be only half as much of me as I am when I am with him."

That's the way God intended it, Jesus would say. We're all in this together—for better, for worse; for richer, for poorer; in sickness and in health. In your life, in your love life—as fathers and mothers, sisters and brothers, husbands and wives, friends and lovers—let us not separate what God has joined together.

❖ SEX IS MADE INTERESTING ❖
THROUGH COMMITMENT

To be honest, Scripture does not have all that much to say about sex—not nearly as much as Hollywood movies or TV sitcoms. While sex is a good gift of God, it is not your whole purpose in life; it is not the defining characteristic of humanity. You were created for joyful service to God and to your neighbor.

For Christians, sex is confined to marriage. It is not to be practiced *before* marriage or *outside* of marriage with someone who is not your spouse. But sex is not nearly as important as fidelity, commitment, and other virtues that make sex interesting. Sex, in itself, is fairly uninteresting. All animals do it. Sex requires about as much intelligence and skill as eating and sleeping.

We make sex interesting through our commitments, through our promises to be with someone forever. Even as God in Jesus Christ has committed to us, so we are able, through the grace of God, to be committed to others.

We make sex interesting through our commitments, through our promises to be with someone forever.

When you come to church to be married, the minister does not ask you in the marriage service, "Have you had sex?" Rather, the pastor asks, "Are you ready to make a promise to love this person, no matter what, forever?" Through these bold promises of marriage, sex becomes interesting, deep, forever fulfilling, and life giving.

This evening, if you call home to your parents and say,

"Guess what? I read a book today," one of them may ask, "What did you read about?" Then, when you say, "I read about sex," your Mom or Dad may ask, "What did the book say about it?"

We hope that you will then reply, "The book said that God invented it, that He's in favor of it, and that He declared that it is real good. But it also said that sex can be terribly abused and that Christians believe that doing it the way God intended makes all the difference."

WHAT ABOUT PENTECOSTALISM?

10

WHAT ABOUT PENTECOSTALISM?

**There are some really lovely people on campus
who call themselves charismatic Christians and are
into "speaking in tongues." I've heard them do it,
and it sounds like a lot of mumbo jumbo to me.
They're into something they call "spiritual warfare,"
and they tell me that if I'm not "Spirit filled,"
demonic forces will destroy me. I'm really confused.**

Sooner or later, you're going to run into Pentecostalism. At even the most sophisticated of universities, you will encounter groups of Christians who claim to have had a special infilling of the Pentecostal gift of the Holy Spirit. Pentecostal Christianity is sweeping South America and Africa. Harvey Cox, a professor of religion and culture at Harvard University, suggests that Pentecostalism, in one form or another, will be the dominant form of Christianity by the middle of the twenty-first century. Meeting up with Pentecostals for the first time can be confusing and even threatening to the more conventional Christians on campus.

Because some Christians refuse to believe that there could be any dimension of the Christian experience that is not a part of their own lives, they react with severe condemnation to the

Pentecostal claim of a special blessing from God. They act as though people who enjoy a gift of the Holy Spirit that they have not experienced are, at best, emotionally disturbed and, at worst, demon possessed. Then there are those Christians who declare that things like speaking in tongues, divine healings, or what Pentecostals call "signs and wonders" may have happened in the earliest days of Christianity; but now, with the completion of the New Testament canon, such works of the Spirit are no longer needed, nor are they a part of authentic Christianity. Citing 1 Corinthians 13:10, "but when the complete comes, the partial will come to an end," they contend that the New Testament is the perfect and complete validation of God and that nothing more is needed for the Church of today.

On the other hand, there are some Pentecostals who believe that if you don't speak in tongues, you really haven't experienced God's presence in your life. These somewhat extremist Pentecostals claim that not having the ability to speak in tongues is evidence that the Holy Spirit is not in you and, therefore, you are not saved.

Fortunately, extremists on both ends of the continuum of religious experiences are becoming increasingly rare. Both the rabid fundamentalists who condemn Pentecostals and the extreme Pentecostals who consign to false religion any who are not into their thing are dying breeds. Healthier and more gracious attitudes have emerged on both sides of the divide. A

Pentecostal friend of ours expressed this more moderate and humble attitude when he said, "Speaking in tongues and having the charismatic experience does not necessarily make me a better Christian than you, but it has helped me to be a better Christian than I was before my charismatic experience." Many noncharismatic Christians, even some Southern Baptist fundamentalists, are ready to admit that there might be "different strokes for different folks" and that Pentecostals are not such a bad lot after all. In short, a gentle peace seems to be emerging in which those on both sides are beginning to affirm

Don't fear encounters with Christians who seem to be different from you.

that there is real Christianity among those who are different from themselves. Both sides are gradually becoming secure enough to be comfortable around one another.

Don't fear encounters with Christians who seem to be different from you, and don't define yourself as spiritually inferior if they experience the presence of the Holy Spirit in their lives in ways quite unlike your own. It is the nature of the Christian faith to be rich, diverse, and multifaceted (sometimes maddeningly so). Never forget that we have four Gospels rather than one. The experience of the risen Christ is so rich that it takes Matthew, Mark, Luke, and John to do justice to Jesus. Try to be open to the possibility that there may be more to the Christian life than you have experienced, and realize none of us yet has *all* the blessings God has in store for us.

❖ A LITTLE BIT OF HISTORY ❖

Pentecostals themselves discern nuances that enable them to differentiate between *kinds* of Pentecostalism. You will hear Pentecostals talk about the differences between those in the old Assemblies of God Churches, that seem heir to the original burst of Pentecostalism in the twentieth century, and the more modern expressions of the movement that utilize such desig-nations as the neo-pentecostal movement and the charismatic movement. Expressions of Pentecostalism in mainline denomi-nations and in the Roman Catholic Church (and yes, Pentecostalism is present in all of them) often come under the name Renewal movement. For all of their claimed differences, they hold much in common.

It all got started in the early part of the twentieth century, when an African-American preacher named William Joseph Seymour started holding special evangelistic services and prayer meetings in a clapboard building in Southern California, known as the Azusa Street Mission. Unusual things began to happen in the course of those meetings, such as people praying and worshiping God in what they called "tongues." To outsiders these utterances sounded like bab-blings and were devoid of any meaning. But to those who were "in the Spirit," they were expressions of love for God and a means of praying that communicated thoughts and feelings too profound and intense to be put into normal language. What was even more unusual to the noninitiated was that, in the highly racist and segregated society of the day, African-Americans and Caucasians were integrated in worship services and evidencing a special love for each other. Onlookers were able to say, "See how they love one another." This love in Christ that crossed the racial divide caused a sensation, and it was not long before that oneness in love drew curious onlookers from far and wide. From these humble beginnings, the Pentecostal movement was underway.

It is worth emphasizing that, in those early days of Pentecostalism, William Seymour declared that the racial unity evident in Pentecostal meetings was the most important evidence that the Holy Spirit was richly present among them and that praying in tongues was secondary. It remained for later Pentecostals to hold up the tongues phenomenon as the defining evidence that a person was "filled with the Holy Spirit." Out of this early movement came an array of new churches and denominations, the most prominent of which was the Assemblies of God.

Up until the late fifties and early sixties, the Pentecostal movement seemed to be little more than a sectarian sideshow, but then things changed rapidly. Signs of Pentecostalism began to emerge in mainline churches. Many Christians in these denominations—tired of a steady diet of overly rational, flat, moralizing preaching and teaching on social justice issues and personal morality—longed for something of God that they could *feel*. Caught up in the civil rights movement and the anti-war movement of the sixties, the leaders of these churches realized they had neglected the subjective, experiential side of Christianity. Many who were hungry for ecstasy in the Spirit and who wanted inner assurance of the presence of God in their lives found the power they were looking for in Pentecostalism, also known as the charismatic renewal movement.

Today, Pentecostal churches are the fastest growing churches in most communities. In mainline denominations, where declines in church membership seem everywhere evident, those congregations that have been impacted by **Pentecostal churches are the fastest growing churches in most communities.** Pentecostalism are usually able to hold their own and, in many instances, demonstrate dynamic growth. In countries like Australia, New Zealand, and those nations that make up the United Kingdom, there is evidence that Christianity is dying a quick death, *except* among Pentecostal churches. In Latin America, Africa, and Asia, the growth of Pentecostalism is well on its way to becoming the dominant form of Christianity in the Third World. In Brazil, on any given Sunday, more people are in Pentecostal churches than in all the more traditional churches combined. And in Honduras, Pentecostal Christianity is fast becoming the overwhelming favorite of the people. No matter where you go these days, you can't escape it. You had better get ready to encounter Pentecostalism. Perhaps, you already have.

✧ PRAYING IN TONGUES VERSUS ✧ SPEAKING IN TONGUES

Before we go any further, we think it best to define some terms and explain what Pentecostals are talking about when they refer to such things as "speaking in tongues," "having the gift of prophecy," "having a word from the Lord," and "praying in tongues." There is no doubt that Pentecostals have developed a system of religious lingo that leaves those outside their fold somewhat confused and more than a bit intimidated. Some clarifications about Pentecostal terminology are essential if the rest of us are to know what they are talking about.

Praying in Tongues

When Pentecostals talk about "speaking in tongues," they usually aren't referring to *speaking* in tongues at all, but rather to *praying* in tongues. Speaking in tongues is useless unless there is someone around who has the gift of interpretation (1 Corinthians 14:27). Such is not the case for *praying* in tongues. Praying in tongues is simply an ecstatic way of expressing love and yearnings for God that are too deep to be put into the common, prosaic language of the culture. It is as if our usual, merely rational language cannot carry the weight of our expansive love of Christ. Some new, ecstatic language of praise is required. In tongues, that language is given.

The sounds made are not meant to be interpreted because they are not a message from God. Instead these "words" are "groanings" from the heart of the Christian who is praying. They are feelings expressed to God, and the sounds are to be understood and appreciated only by God.

Paul writes: "Likewise the Spirit helps us in our weakness; for we do not know how to pray as we ought, but that very Spirit intercedes with sighs too deep for words. And God, who searches the heart, knows what is the mind of the Spirit, because the Spirit intercedes for the saints according to the will of God" (Romans 8:26–27).

When Christians pray in tongues, they believe that the Holy Spirit prays *through* them. In other words, praying in tongues is the Holy Spirit flowing through the Christian and giving praise to the Father, carrying the Christian's unarticulated emotions and needs to God the Father. According to Pentecostals, praying in tongues occurs when Christians allow something from the depths of their being to flow out and upward toward God. Praying in tongues is not meant for understanding, and it is not meant to add knowledge to the church. Again, Paul writes: "For if I pray in a tongue, my spirit prays, but my mind is unproductive" (1 Corinthians 14:14).

Speaking in Tongues

Speaking in tongues occurs when an individual becomes a "mouthpiece for God" and has a special message from God for the Church. The "words" that such a person utters are in an "unknown heavenly language." The apostle Paul contends that when a person is exercising this gift, someone with the gift of interpretation must be on hand to translate the message (1 Corinthians 12:10; 14:13). Otherwise, all we have is vain babbling: Paul says, "If anyone speaks in a tongue, let there be only two or at most three, and each in turn; and let one interpret. But if there is no one to interpret, let them be silent in church and speak to themselves and to God.... For God is a God not of disorder but of peace" (1 Corinthians 14:27–28, 33).

❖ THE GIFTS OF THE SPIRIT VERSUS ❖ THE FRUIT OF THE SPIRIT

The next thing to clarify is the difference between the *gifts* of the Spirit and the *fruit* of the Spirit.

The Gifts of the Spirit

When the Bible speaks of "the gifts of the Spirit," it is referring to special talents and abilities God gives to Christians so they can provide for the Church all the power, love, and commitment needed for it to carry out its mission. The Church needs preachers, so, according to the Scriptures, God gives to the Church people who have the gift of preaching. The Church needs teachers to provide clarity concerning the essential doctrines of the faith, so God provides people with special teaching gifts to meet that need. The Church needs missionaries (i.e., apostles) and evangelists to win converts, and the Bible teaches that we can count on God to raise up people who have the gifts to fulfill these ministries. Concerning the gifts of the Spirit, the Book of Ephesians says:

> The gifts he gave were that some would be apostles, some prophets, some evangelists, some pastors and teachers, to equip the saints for the work of ministry, for building up the body of Christ, until all of us come to the unity of the faith and of the knowledge of the Son of God, to maturity, to the measure of the full stature of Christ. (Ephesians 4:11–13)

Not all of these gifts are spectacular in nature. Actually, the apostle Paul makes a strong point that those who have the "up-front" gifts that get public recognition may not be the most important in the life and maintenance of the Church: "On the contrary, the members of the body that seem to be weaker are indispensable, and those members of the body that we think less honorable we clothe with greater honor, and our less respectable members are treated with greater respect" (1 Corinthians 12:22–23).

All of us who are a part of the Church know people who are essential to the ministries of the Church but who are not good up-front people. Some are especially gifted in conflict resolution and make excellent moderators for church business meetings. Others have a gift for hospitality and are able to set up those church sup-pers that are so important in building a sense of community among the members. Still others are good at one-on-one relation-ships and are brilliant at counseling people in times of trouble. It is a mistake to suggest that only those who preach have a special call-ing from God. *All of us* are called to use whatever gifts

> *All of us are called to use whatever gifts or talents God has given us.*

or talents God has given us to build up the Church so she can carry out her mission in the world. The tendency to mystify the calling of the preacher and make it unique is a distortion of the biblical message that each of us is called to serve the world through the Church (Ephesians 1:22–23) and that each of us is to discern how she or he can best minister according to the gift that each has been given.

The Fruit of the Spirit

Indeed, there are, as the Scriptures say, "varieties of gifts" in the body of Christ. But the Bible also refers to the *fruit* of the Spirit, which is manifested in qualities of personality that are increasingly evident in the lives of those who are becoming sanctified Christians. The fruit of the Spirit is evidenced in the traits of those who yield themselves to the kind of transformation God wants to bring about in God's people. When, after making a commitment to Christ, a person becomes discipled into a godly lifestyle and seeks to grow into the likeness of Christ, certain changes begin to take place. Regular prayer, Bible study, and meditation on a personal level, coupled with serving the poor and standing up for the oppressed on the societal level, effect a metamorphosis for the Christian. According to Galatians 5, the following qualities become increasingly evident in the person's life: "By contrast, the fruit of the Spirit is love, joy, peace, patience, kindness, generosity, faithfulness, gentleness, and self-control. There is no law against such things" (Galatians 5:22–23).

Having the *fruit* of the Spirit is much more important than having the *gifts* of the Spirit.

The apostle Paul makes it clear that having the *fruit* of the Spirit is more important than having the *gifts* of the Spirit. This is a major theme of the well-known "Love Chapter," 1 Corinthians 13. After discussing the variety of spiritual gifts, Paul tells us that love is the primary fruit of the Spirit. Love is more important than *any* of the gifts. From this passage it is evident that love is the ultimate gift from God and the most important trait a Christian can have: "If I speak in the tongues of mortals and of angels, but do not have love, I am a noisy gong or a clanging cymbal. And if I have prophetic powers, and understand all mysteries and all knowledge, and if I have all faith, so as to remove mountains, but do not have love, I am nothing" (1 Corinthians 13:1–2).

The Gifts and Fruit Aren't a Package Deal

It should be noted that sometimes those with the *gifts* of the Spirit are painfully lacking in the *fruit* of the Spirit. The personal possession of the gifts of the Spirit appears to have little to do with whether or not a person demonstrates love toward others. The Spirit that is given is the Spirit of Jesus, the one who fully demonstrates the fruit of the Spirit through sacrificial works of love. The fact that someone can preach up a storm or heal the sick is not an indicator of that person's spiritual condition. Unfortunately, the gifts and the fruit do not necessarily go together.

One of the most painful realizations of Tony's seminary days was that some of the most gifted preachers gave little evidence of possessing the fruit of the Spirit. Many of those great preachers went on to become big-name leaders of large churches. On the other hand, Tony knew many people whose personal holiness was a thing of beauty, but because they lacked the gift of preaching, they were consigned to small churches "in the sticks," where few would ever hear them. For reasons that we find hard to understand, God sometimes gives gifts to people who show few signs of being "spiritual" and leaves those who obviously "walk in the Spirit" with very few of the abilities needed to be outstanding leaders of the Church.

J. Edwin Orr, the Irish revivalist, told of an evangelist who was a very gifted preacher. This evangelist became involved in an adulterous affair with the piano player on his crusade team. One night the song leader of the team accidentally walked into a bedroom where he found the evangelist and the piano player in an extremely compromising situation. Shocked, the song leader shouted at the pair and told them how disgusted he was. With only one night left of the evangelistic crusade they were conducting, the song leader agreed to lead the singing one last time; but then he would be finished with the team forever.

The next night, the corrupt evangelist preached brilliantly. The lusts of the flesh, which had taken control of him, seemed to provide little, if any, hindrance to his homiletic effectiveness. That night he seemed more effective than ever.

When the invitation was given for people to come down the aisle and give their lives to Christ, the response was over-whelming. Hundreds responded to the altar call. As the choir was singing the invitation hymn and the people were stream-ing forward, the evangelist leaned toward the song leader and asked arrogantly, "Well, how am I doing?"

There is no question that this sinful man had the gift of

evangelism. There is no doubt that most of the people converted that night had a genuine experience with God. Yet it is just as certain that the evangelist lacked spirituality and was mired in the lusts of the flesh.

This true story goes to show that God can draw straight lines with crooked sticks. God will use whom God will use. God is sovereign, and though we don't understand it, we must accept that God will give the gifts of the Spirit to whom He chooses.

Having certain gifts of the Spirit may give those who possess them fame and recognition, but having the *fruit* of the Spirit is its own reward.

CONCLUSION

CONCLUSION

The End?

There's something a bit presumptuous about ending a book on being a Christian. We have not given you a complete guide to absolutely everything that a Christian needs to know. This faith—its beliefs and its practices—is large. You can spend a very long lifetime as a friend of Jesus and still be surprised by Him. We can't—even if we had the insight and the intelligence, even if we had a thousand more pages—explain it all for you. As a friend of ours enjoys saying to students who think they have a handle on God, "If you can explain it, it probably isn't God."

There's an even bigger problem with ending a book like this on a subject like discipleship. Discipleship is not a matter of ending; it's always beginning. Jesus told us to "turn and become as a child." Maybe, in this matter of following Jesus, we are all beginners. The point is not to arrive at that point where you can smugly declare, "I've got it!" The point is to be willing to grow, to travel with Jesus, to go on a journey with Jesus that is called salvation.

Perhaps that's why Jesus told so many stories, so many parables, that don't really have an ending. When He told the story of the prodigal son, Jesus didn't tell us if, after the party for the returning son, they all lived happily ever after. At the end of his great story of the Good Samaritan, Jesus didn't tell us how the injured man and the Samaritan got on after the event. Perhaps Jesus didn't give a complete ending to so many of these stories because we are supposed to finish them ourselves, in our own lives, in our daily walk with Jesus. So most parables are not about the end, the completion of our journey with Jesus, but rather invitations to begin or encouragements to continue.

Perhaps that's why the primary way the gospels present Jesus with his disciples is as people on a journey. Jesus is always moving quickly from place to place, with his poor, sometimes dazed and confused disciples stumbling along after Him. He calls disciples, not to sit down and rest with Him, not to build great stone buildings where they can settle down with Him; rather He calls disciples to move with Him, to keep walking behind Him, to stay on the way with Him. In fact, the Acts of the Apostles says that the very first Christians called themselves The Way.

We have written this book to help you along the way. These words, as helpful as we hope they will be, are not the way. Jesus is the way, the truth, and the life. You are a person who has begun to walk that way. You are not at the destination, not yet, but you are on the way. God's blessings upon you as you continue to grow in Christ, as you continue to live out the implications of your decision to walk with Jesus, as you daily discover the adventure of discipleship. We are confident that you will not simply survive, but that you will triumph and have life abundantly.

The thing that makes you special and that gives us hope is that, when you heard Jesus say, "Follow me," you knew that He meant you and you dared to follow.

The beginning.

DISCUSSION QUESTIONS

Chapter 1: HOW DO I KNOW IF I'M A CHRISTIAN?

1. To what extent do you consider yourself a Christian? What about you contributes to a positive answer to this question, and what contributes to a negative answer?

2. Do we have the right to set up criteria to make judgments about whether other people are Christians, and if not, how do we determine who should be admitted into church membership?

Chapter 2: HOW CAN I READ THE BIBLE AND GET SOMETHING OUT OF IT?

1. To what extent do you think that the Bible is infallible? What difference does it make whether it is or is not?

2. What are the principles that guide you as you try to interpret the Bible in today's world?

Chapter 3: DO I HAVE TO GO TO CHURCH TO BE A GOOD CHRISTIAN?

1. Is faithfulness in the life of a church really crucial for Christians, or can a person be Christian without being a part of a regularly meeting group of believers?

2. Should we do away with denominationalism, or are denominational distinctives important?

Chapter 4: AM I A SINNER?

1. Is the authors' definition of sin too simplistic, or is there more to it than they suggest?

2. Can you come up with some examples of your own of corporate sin?

Chapter 5: HOW DO I KNOW WHAT'S RIGHT?

1. Many people these days are wearing WWJD (What Would Jesus Do) pins. Do you think that asking that question in every situation will enable you to resolve *every* ethical dilemma.

2. St. Augustine once said, "Love God and do as you please." What are the implications of that statement?

Chapter 6: AM I SUPPOSED TO TRY TO CONVERT PEOPLE TO CHRISTIANITY?

1. Can you give good and bad examples of how Christians have tried to share their faith commitments with others?

2. What do you think is the eternal destiny of those who never accept Jesus as Lord, Savior, and God? On what do you base your answer?

Chapter 7: HOW CAN I LISTEN TO A SERMON AND GET SOMETHING OUT OF IT?

1. Do you have a favorite preacher? If you do, what makes that preacher special to you?

2. Can you think of sermons that impacted you in a positive manner? How did they impact you, and why?

3. Can you think of sermons that impacted you in a negative manner? How did they impact you, and why?

Discussion Questions

Chapter 8: WHAT'S THE POINT OF WORSHIP?

1. Will loves liturgy. At his services at the Duke University Chapel, those into traditional worship are thrilled. But what about the contemporary worship services that are now in vogue? Do you prefer them to traditional worship?

2. How does the new "praise music" that typifies contemporary worship compare with the traditional and often classical music of the church? What do these different types of music do to you spiritually?

Chapter 9: AND WHAT ABOUT SEX?

1. Tony has said jokingly that as a boy he was told that sex was a dirty, filthy thing—and that you should save it for the person you marry. Do you believe, as some do, that Christianity has promoted a view of sex that has harmed people emotionally and over the years has had a detrimental influence on marriages?

2. What do you think the Bible says about premarital sex, and what do you think about it?

Chapter 10: WHAT ABOUT PENTECOSTALISM?

1. Does Pentecostalism frighten you? If so, why? If not, why not?

2. Do you perceive "speaking in tongues" as a lot of emotionalism or as a genuine spiritual experience? And do you see it as hurtful or helpful to the future of Christianity?